Church and State

Other Books in the History of Issues Series

THE HISTORY OF ISSUES

Church and State

Robert Winters, Book Editor

GREENHAVEN PRESS
A part of Gale, Cengage Learning

GALE
CENGAGE Learning™

Detroit • New York • San Francisco • New Haven, Conn • Waterville, Maine • London

Christine Nasso, *Publisher*
Elizabeth Des Chenes, *Managing Editor*

© 2008 Greenhaven Press, a part of Gale, Cengage Learning

Gale and Greenhaven Press are registered trademarks used herein under license.

For more information, contact:
Greenhaven Press
27500 Drake Rd.
Farmington Hills, MI 48331-3535
Or you can visit our Internet site at gale.cengage.com

Articles in Greenhaven Press anthologies are often edited for length to meet page requirements. In addition, original titles of these works are changed to clearly present the main thesis and to explicitly indicate the author's opinion. Every effort is made to ensure that Greenhaven Press accurately reflects the original intent of the authors. Every effort has been made to trace the owners of copyrighted material.

Cover image copyright Mikhail Levit, 2008. Used under license from Shutterstock.com.

LIBRARY OF CONGRESS CATALOGING-IN-PUBLICATION DATA

Church and state / Robert Winters, book editor.
    p. cm. -- (History of issues)
    Includes bibliographical references and index.
    ISBN 978-0-7377-3970-1 (hardcover)
    1. Church and state--United States. 2. Christianity and politics--United States.
    3. United States--Church history. I. Winters, Robert, 1963-
    BR516.C485 2008
    322'.10973--dc22
                                           2008021500

Printed in the United States of America
1 2 3 4 5 6 7 12 11 10 09 08

Contents

Chapter 1: Early Thoughts on Religion and Government

Chapter 2: Church and State in the New Republic

Baptists quickly embrace the idea that taxation and other methods of forcing them to support religions that they disagree with are as unfair as the taxation without representation that helped launch the American Revolution.

Chapter 3: The Intersection of Government and Religion

Chapter 4: The Wall of Separation and Its Opponents

Foreword

In the 1940s, at the height of the Holocaust, Jews struggled to create a nation of their own in Palestine, a region of the Middle East that at the time was controlled by Britain. The British had placed limits on Jewish immigration to Palestine, hampering efforts to provide refuge to Jews fleeing the Holocaust. In response to this and other British policies, an underground Jewish resistance group called Irgun began carrying out terrorist attacks against British targets in Palestine, including immigration, intelligence, and police offices. Most famously, the group bombed the King David Hotel in Jerusalem, the site of a British military headquarters. Although the British were warned well in advance of the attack, they failed to evacuate the building. As a result, ninety-one people were killed (including fifteen Jews) and forty-five were injured.

Early in the twentieth century, Ireland, which had long been under British rule, was split into two countries. The south, populated mostly by Catholics, eventually achieved independence and became the Republic of Ireland. Northern Ireland, mostly Protestant, remained under British control. Catholics in both the north and south opposed British control of the north, and the Irish Republican Army (IRA) sought unification of Ireland as an independent nation. In 1969, the IRA split into two factions. A new radical wing, the Provisional IRA, was created and soon undertook numerous terrorist bombings and killings throughout Northern Ireland, the Republic of Ireland, and even in England. One of its most notorious attacks was the 1974 bombing of a Birmingham, England, bar that killed nineteen people.

In the mid-1990s, an Islamic terrorist group called al Qaeda began carrying out terrorist attacks against American targets overseas. In communications to the media, the organization listed several complaints against the United States. It generally opposed all U.S. involvement and presence in the Middle East. It particularly objected to the presence of U.S. troops in Saudi Arabia, which is the home of several Islamic holy sites. And it strongly condemned the United States for supporting the nation of Israel, which it claimed was an oppressor of Muslims. In 1998 al Qaeda's leaders issued a fatwa (a religious legal statement) calling for Muslims to kill Americans. Al Qaeda acted on this order many times—most memorably on September 11, 2001, when it attacked the World Trade Center and the Pentagon, killing nearly three thousand people.

These three groups—Irgun, the Provisional IRA, and al Qaeda—have achieved varied results. Irgun's terror campaign contributed to Britain's decision to pull out of Palestine and to support the creation of Israel in 1948. The Provisional IRA's tactics kept pressure on the British, but they also alienated many would-be supporters of independence for Northern Ireland. Al Qaeda's attacks provoked a strong U.S. military response but did not lessen America's involvement in the Middle East nor weaken its support of Israel. Despite these different results, the means and goals of these groups were similar. Although they emerged in different parts of the world during different eras and in support of different causes, all three had one thing in common: They all used clandestine violence to undermine a government they deemed oppressive or illegitimate.

The destruction of oppressive governments is not the only goal of terrorism. For example, terror is also used to minimize dissent in totalitarian regimes and to promote extreme ideologies. However, throughout history the motivations of terrorists have been remarkably similar, proving the old adage that "the more things change, the more they remain the same." Arguments for and against terrorism thus boil down to the same set of universal arguments regardless of the age: Some argue that terrorism is justified to change (or, in the case of state terror, to maintain) the prevailing political order; others respond that terrorism is inhumane and unacceptable under any circumstances. These basic views transcend time and place.

Similar fundamental arguments apply to other controversial social issues. For instance, arguments over the death penalty have always featured competing views of justice. Scholars cite biblical texts to claim that a person who takes a life must forfeit his or her life, while others cite religious doctrine to support their view that only God can take a human life. These arguments have remained essentially the same throughout the centuries. Likewise, the debate over euthanasia has persisted throughout the history of Western civilization. Supporters argue that it is compassionate to end the suffering of the dying by hastening their impending death; opponents insist that it is society's duty to make the dying as comfortable as possible as death takes its natural course.

Greenhaven Press's *The History of Issues* series illustrates this constancy of arguments surrounding major social issues. Each volume in the series focuses on one issue—including terrorism, the death penalty, and euthanasia—and examines how the debates have both evolved and remained essentially the same over the years. Primary documents such as newspaper articles, speeches, and government reports illuminate historical developments and offer perspectives from throughout history. Secondary sources provide overviews and commentaries from a more contemporary perspective. An introduction begins each anthology and supplies essential context and background. An annotated table of contents, chronology, and index allow for easy reference, and a bibliography and list of organizations to contact point to additional sources of information on the book's topic. With these features, *The History of Issues* series permits readers to glimpse both the historical and contemporary dimensions of humanity's most pressing and controversial social issues.

Introduction

Article VI of the U.S. Constitution guarantees that "no religious test shall ever be required as a Qualification to any Office or public Trust under the United States." For some, this is a definitive answer to whether religion should play a part in elections. In fact, however, the American electorate can have any test it wants, and in practice, religion has often been one of the tests that voters use to pick a president. Throughout the nineteenth century, religion was the best predictor of voter preference, along with ethnicity, which was itself closely tied to religion. It is not that religious questions were always central. Instead, religion provided a fundamental loyalty to particular parties and policies that was very difficult to break through.

Election of 1800

Thomas Jefferson was the first to feel the intensity of religious fervor in the pivotal election of 1800. The more conservative Federalist Party had dominated the young republic since its birth in 1789. However, laws like the Alien and Sedition Acts, which sought to suppress criticism of the John Adams administration, had only increased that opposition. Many people sought a real change, and Jefferson's party offered that change. The Federalists knew they were in trouble, but they did have one major issue.

Jefferson had written a number of letters denying such central Christian doctrines as the divinity of Jesus and the Virgin Birth. Although he never formally laid out his own beliefs, it was well known that he leaned toward Deism, the belief that God had created the universe and the physical laws but did not directly intervene in the affairs of the world. He was also known as an early supporter of the French Revolution, which had gone from a fairly conservative attempt to limit the monarchy to a radical and violent attempt to completely remake society. This had included mass executions of aristocrats, the burning of churches, and the murder of thousands of priests and nuns as well as ordinary French citizens who refused to give up their religion.

The Federalists, especially the pro-Federalist clergy in New England, seized on both of these to paint Jefferson as a dangerous atheist who sought to destroy religion in America. Even before the campaign, in 1798, Thomas Dwight, the president of Yale University and a prominent Federalist, was denouncing the prospect of a Jefferson candidacy. If Jefferson won, he declared, "We may see the Bible cast into a bonfire, the vessels of the sacramental supper borne by an ass in public procession, and our children, either wheedled or terrified, uniting in chanting mockeries against God." During the campaign itself, the pro-Federalist *Gazette of the United States*, put the question bluntly: "Shall I continue in allegiance to God— and a Religious President; Or impiously declare for Jefferson—and No God!!!"

In the end, Jefferson defeated the Federalists so thoroughly that they had ceased to operate as a national party by the 1820s. A profound bitterness remained in New England, but even there the clergy were losing their influence, and one by one the New England states disestablished their churches. Jefferson himself made a point of attending church services as president, somewhat defusing the issue, and neither of his successors, James Madison nor James Monroe, caused the kind of religious outrage that Jefferson had. The issue faded from the national scene, but an odd incident showed that it could revive quite unexpectedly and powerfully.

The Anti-Masonic Party

Freemasonry had been closely bound up with the birth of the American Republic and counted Benjamin Franklin, Paul Revere, and George Washington as members. Washington himself had presided over a Masonic ceremony laying the corner-stone of the U.S. Capitol and was given a Masonic funeral in 1799. Along with these American heroes, however, Freemasonry was also associated with secrecy, elitism, and secular values. For some Americans, especially among the evangelical churches, this was a dangerous combination.

In 1826 in Batavia, New York, an estranged Mason by the name of William Morgan announced that he was going to publish a book revealing the secrets of Freemasonry. Prominent Freemasons moved quickly, declaring that he owed them money, and had him arrested and placed in debtors' prison. Shortly thereafter, somebody claiming to be a friend paid Morgan's debt and took him away in a carriage. He was not seen again.

Morgan's disappearance sparked fear and outrage throughout upstate New York and rapidly spread to other states. In churches and revival meetings, preachers denounced the Freemasons, declaring that they were preparing to murder their opponents as a first step toward a government takeover. This movement grew into the Anti-Masonic Party, America's first third party, and soon attracted the attention of prominent politicians. Most important of these was President John Quincy Adams, who was seeking reelection in 1828 against Andrew Jackson, who was a high-ranking Mason. Adams lost, but the party remained as an anti-Jacksonian force in politics and eventually merged with other Jackson opponents to form the Whig Party.

The passions that created the Anti-Masonic Party faded as rapidly as they began, and by 1836 it had ceased to be an independent political party. It did, however, clearly reveal that religious feeling remained a potentially powerful force in national politics. It also had an interesting legacy. It was the first party to hold a national convention to nominate its presidential and vice-presidential candidates, an innovation adopted by every party since.

Catholics and Protestants

Fear of secret Masonic conspiracies has never entirely evaporated in the United States, but it did not last long as a force in electoral politics. Far more pervasive and long-lasting was the fear and dislike of the Catholic Church and Catholic immigrants. In fact, a number of veterans of the Anti-Masonic Party found themselves drawn to anti-Catholic politics as waves of German and Irish Catholic immigrants reached America in the 1840s and 1850s. Ironically, the groups that came together in this effort embraced the kind of secrecy that had originally outraged the Anti-Masons. Members of the emerging movement were told to say "I know nothing" whenever asked about their political activities, and they were soon known semi-officially as the Know Nothings.

The Know Nothings flourished for a while, winning elections in cities like Boston, Chicago, and Washington, D.C., and capturing the state government of Massachusetts, but they soon disappeared as a party. Instead, antislavery Know Nothings joined the newborn Republican Party to help elect Abraham Lincoln in 1860. The Civil War, the end of slavery, and Reconstruction easily overshadowed the religious issues that had once motivated Know Nothings and like-minded Republicans. However, they laid the groundwork for a division that would help shape much of the nation's history for the next hundred years.

The triumphant Republicans who had won the Civil War and freed the slaves were overwhelmingly northern Protestants descended from British settlers. In contrast, the "outsiders," mainly Catholic and Jewish immigrants in the northern cities and white southern Protestants who deeply resented the Civil War and the era of Reconstruction, found themselves in an uneasy alliance in the Democratic Party. African Americans generally voted Republican for the rest of the nineteenth and much of the twentieth century.

Rum, Romanism, and Rebellion

A remark by James G. Blaine, the Republican nominee for president in 1884, summed up the attitude of the northern Protestant establishment. In the middle of the campaign, he denounced the Democratic Party as the party of "Rum, Romanism, and Rebellion." He was referring to this alliance of northern Roman Catholics, who controlled a number of political machines in big cities, with the southern Protestants who had tried to secede from the Union a generation earlier and continued to fight bitterly against any attempt to give African Americans full equality. The reference to rum was somewhat more complicated.

There was a strong evangelical element in the Republican Party, as there had been in the abolitionist movement that helped create the party. With slavery gone, many turned their attention to other issues of poverty and oppression, and many came to believe that alcohol was a big part of the problem. They blamed it for unemployment, wife beating, divorce, child abandonment, sickness, and many other things that certainly were made worse, though not entirely caused, by alcoholism. Their answer was to outlaw alcohol, an answer Democrats resisted, especially since Republicans often framed it as part of an overall attack on the "vices" of immigrants.

Blaine's remark perfectly captured a moment in which the dominant political party saw its opposition as superstitious alcoholics, traitors, and foreigners, and above all, losers. His defeat in the election showed that that moment was a passing one. Both parties began to settle down into somewhat more broad-based coalitions, with Republicans drawing at least some Catholics into their ranks and Democrats attracting more evangelicals. In fact, in 1896 the Democrats nominated William Jennings Bryan, an evangelical Christian reformer and populist, for president.

America seemed to have adopted a kind of religious truce, which some historians have called an American civic religion.

Under this, many Protestants, Catholics, and Jews accepted the basic premise that religion was best kept private. At the same time, members of all churches were expected to uphold the basic premises of the U.S. Constitution, including the separation of church and state. That did not mean religion was kept out of public life. Instead, there was a general embrace of semireligious concepts such as the idea that the United States is God's chosen country and that as a nation Americans owe their rights and freedoms to God. Behind this was a general consensus that politics and religion in fact could mix but only in the sense that Americans were united under one God, and political fights over religious doctrines were un-American.

From Al Smith to John F. Kennedy

The limits to that consensus became clear in 1928 when the Democrats nominated the Catholic governor of New York, Alfred E. "Al" Smith, for president. The first non-Protestant to win the endorsement of a major party, Smith continually faced the accusation that he would answer to the pope if elected. Since he was a New Yorker, the charge of "rebellion" did not apply, but "rum and Romanism" were once again flung at this opponent of Prohibition.

Southerners within his own Democratic Party, even some senators, viciously attacked him and all Catholics as dangerous enemies of American Protestant values. The Ku Klux Klan, a powerful force at the time, printed thousands of anti-Smith pamphlets. One even claimed that a secret tunnel connected the Vatican and New York City. Mainstream Protestant churches and establishment leaders made no attempt to counter these charges, and many actively encouraged them. In the end, Smith lost to Herbert Hoover in a landslide.

It was a sharp warning to anyone who thought that religious divisions were disappearing. They were, however, about to be completely overshadowed, replaced by the Great Depression and World War II. The Depression doomed the reelection chances of Herbert Hoover and plunged the nation into one of its gravest crises ever. People of all faiths and ethnicities found themselves united in seeking relief from poverty and soon after in defeating Nazi Germany and the Japanese Empire. After fighting against ideologies of hatred and exclusion, it seemed that Americans were ready to embrace the unity of the civic religion more than ever. This attitude was summed up by President Dwight D. Eisenhower: "Our form of government has no sense unless it is founded in a deeply felt religious faith, and I don't care what it is."

Again, that attitude would prove to be an illusion. In 1960, the Democrats once again nominated a Catholic, John F. Kennedy, for president. Throughout the primary battles, he was routinely attacked, much as Smith had been, as someone who, if he became president, would have to answer to the pope. Having won the nomination, he decided to address these fears directly in a speech to a group of ministers in Houston, Texas, on September 12, about two months before the election. The speech clearly outlined Kennedy's commitment to separation of church and state but also stoutly attacked the idea that somebody's religion could make them ineligible to be president. Kennedy won in a very narrow victory, and undoubtedly many voted either for or against him based largely on his religion. Nevertheless, that victory has been seen as a major turning point in the history of religion in America by breaking the hold that mainstream Protestantism had had on the presidency.

Since Kennedy

Since then, the question of religion in presidential elections has been more muted. There is a general sense, in the media and the populace, that questioning of the kind that Smith and Kennedy had to endure is not quite right. That does not mean it has entirely disappeared. When Michigan governor George Romney, a Mormon, ran for the Republican nomination in

1968 there was some controversy about the fact that the Mormon Church at that time did not admit blacks to its priesthood. Romney's strong civil rights record in his state deflected those concerns, however, and his religion was mostly ignored by reporters and the voters.

In 2000, Joseph Lieberman was picked by Al Gore as his running mate, becoming the first Jew to run on a major party's national ticket. At first, some Jewish organizations worried that his presence on that ticket might spark an anti-Semitic backlash, but that never materialized. In fact, the choice of Lieberman, who was a vocal critic of President Bill Clinton during the Monica Lewinsky sex scandal, was seen as distancing Gore from that scandal and countering claims that the Democratic Party was hostile to traditional morality. At any rate, the Gore-Lieberman ticket won the popular vote, although they lost the electoral vote in one of the most controversial election results in American history.

Oddly, it was George Romney's son Mitt who, in the contest for the 2008 Republican presidential nomination, faced the kind of backlash that had not been seen since the 1960 campaign. There were evangelists who told him bluntly at campaign stops that they would never vote for a Mormon. Evangelical pastors and talk radio hosts decried Mormonism as a cult and Romney as a dangerous choice. For a candidate in the Republican nomination battle, where evangelicals have far more influence than in the Democratic Party, this was a very serious problem.

To answer this growing chorus, Mitt Romney decided to repeat Kennedy's strategy and answer the issue directly in a major speech. There were some differences, however. Unlike Kennedy's deliberately chosen hostile audience, Romney gave his speech to a largely friendly group at the George Bush Presidential Library. He also departed somewhat from the strict separation that Kennedy had embraced, saying instead that the United States seemed to have gone too far in the direction of secularism. Nevertheless, the overall point was the same: that nobody's religion should prevent them from running for president and that no president would answer to his religion's leaders rather than the Constitution. The speech was well received by many evangelicals, some of whom began to prefer him to his rivals for the nomination. Nevertheless, a number of evangelicals voted for Arkansas governor Mike Huckabee, an evangelical pastor, in the primaries, and in the end Romney decided to suspend his campaign and endorse the candidacy of John McCain.

Many factors of course play into the success or failure of a presidential candidate, and it would be far too simplistic to say that being Mormon cost Mitt Romney the nomination. Still, his experience, and that of his rival Mike Huckabee, showed that religious affiliation is still a potentially powerful factor in presidential campaigns. Both candidates also drew a lot of criticism from secular voters, who have been more vocal in recent years than in previous campaigns. For them, calls for national unity behind a genetic civic religion are as offensive as calls for rallying behind any particular religious sect.

THE
HISTORY
OF
ISSUES

CHAPTER 1

Early Thoughts on Religion and Government

Chapter Preface

Separatists, who had given up on maintaining any connection with the Church of England, arrived on the *Mayflower* as Pilgrims in 1620 and established the Plymouth Colony. Puritans, who sought to purify the Church of England of all nonbiblical practices, founded the Massachusetts Bay Colony in 1629. Together, they have profoundly shaped American attitudes toward freedom of religion and the role of churches. Despite fundamental disagreements, both groups recognized that their arrival in the New World gave them an unusual opportunity to establish a new society on religious principles, far from the influence of the king or his bishops. In that sense, they can often be treated as one group, and in fact the Massachusetts Bay Colony absorbed Plymouth Colony in 1691, making for one Puritan-dominated colony.

Unlike the young men seeking fortune and adventure in the new settlements of Virginia, the Puritans settled their colony as entire families, and often entire congregations. This gave them a cohesion and a unity that set them apart, and there was much less intermarriage with native peoples than elsewhere. This unity also made it easier for a small group, led by Governor John Winthrop, to dominate the colony for many decades. Even as democracy expanded, the influence of highly educated clergymen such as John Cotton remained, and most of the settlers accepted that Judeo-Christian principles should underlie the legal system. And only full church members, who had to publicly describe their conversion experience, were allowed to vote. For many, democracy and theocracy (or rule by God—through the clergy) were largely the same thing.

Eventually, of course, tensions developed. Puritan leaders reacted harshly to dissension and often tortured, banished, or executed their opponents. Still, dissension kept cropping up, and some, such as Anne Hutchinson and Roger Williams, spoke out against the control of the Puritan leadership. Williams published eloquent testimonials to religious tolerance and founded his own colony, Rhode Island, as a haven for nonconformists. Time also played a role, as the deeply religious first generation gave way to new generations that lacked the fervor of their ancestors. In 1662, the colony adopted the Halfway Covenant, which provided that the children and grandchildren of church members could obtain a partial membership, without declaring a spiritual experience, and maintain their right to vote. Even these members had to agree to accept church guidelines, however.

Events back in England also played a role. The persecutions that led to the founding of the colony, and continued to supply it with new arrivals, ended during the English Civil War and the Protectorate of Puritan Oliver Cromwell in the 1640s and 1650s. The restoration of King Charles II in 1660 did not cause a return to persecution, but it did create a government that was less sympathetic to Puritan leaders in New England and more likely to favor those seeking to loosen their control. More important, these upheavals, including the overthrow of the Catholic king James II in 1688, caused a number of influential thinkers, especially philosopher John Locke, to advocate for religious tolerance and much greater freedom regarding religion.

The Puritans still retain their grip on the American imagination, although often as a negative example. In truth, they were not nearly as rigid or somber or hostile to sexuality and to pleasure as they are often portrayed to be. They were, however, serious about establishing a society that would be based on biblical principles. Those who see the United States as a nation founded on Christian principles are largely thinking of the Puritans. The idea of the United States as a "city on a hill," a phrase from the Gospels used by Governor John Winthrop to describe the model Christian society, remains very powerful even in a country that officially embraces the separation of church and state.

Forcing Citizens to Accept Religious Doctrines Is Wrong

Roger Williams

Born in London in 1603, Roger Williams came to the Massachu-setts Bay Colony in 1630, where he soon became the pastor of Salem. Almost from the beginning, he found himself in conflict with the colony's government over its treatment of the Native Americans and over the religious authority of the local magis-trates. In 1635, he was banished from the colony and soon estab-lished a new settlement, named Providence, that grew into the colony of Rhode Island. In 1644, while in England seeking a charter for the new colony, he published The Bloudy Tenent of Persecution for Cause of Conscience, *one of the first and most forceful expressions of the idea that freedom of religious belief was a fundamental right. The tract opens with twelve proposi-tions and proceeds as a dialogue between Peace and Truth about these ideas. The following excerpt includes those twelve proposi-tions, radical at the time, and gives a sense of the vigorous de-bate that underlies the entire dialogue.*

First, that the blood of so many hundred thousand souls of Protestants and Papists [Catholics], spilt in the wars of present and former ages, for their respective consciences, is not required nor accepted by Jesus Christ the Prince of Peace.

Secondly, pregnant scriptures and arguments are through-out the work proposed against the doctrine of persecution for cause of conscience.

Thirdly, satisfactory answers are given to scriptures, and objections produced by Mr. [John] Calvin, [Theodore] Beza, Mr. [John] Cotton, and the ministers of the New English churches and others former and later, tending to prove the doctrine of persecution for cause of conscience.

Roger Williams, from *The Bloudy Tenent of Persecution for Cause of Conscience*, 1644, republished in *Publications of the Narragansett Club*, vol. III, Providence, R.I., 1867.

Fourthly, the doctrine of persecution for cause of conscience is proved guilty of all the blood of the souls crying for vengeance under the altar [a reference to Revelation 6:9].

Fifthly, all civil states with their officers of justice in their respective constitutions and administrations are proved essentially civil, and therefore not judges, governors, or defenders of the spiritual or Christian state and worship.

Sixthly, it is the will and command of God that (since the coming of his Son the Lord Jesus) a permission of the most paganish, Jewish, Turkish [that is, Muslim], or antichristian consciences and worships, be granted to all men in all nations and countries; and they are only to be fought against with that sword which is only (in soul matters) able to conquer, to wit, the sword of God's Spirit, the Word of God.

Seventhly, the state of the Land of Israel, the kings and people thereof in peace and war, is proved figurative and ceremonial, and no pattern nor president [precedent] for any kingdom or civil state in the world to follow.

Uniformity Not Required

Eighthly, God requireth not a uniformity of religion to be enacted and enforced in any civil state; which enforced uniformity (sooner or later) is the greatest occasion of civil war, ravishing of conscience, persecution of Christ Jesus in his servants, and of the hypocrisy and destruction of millions of souls.

Ninthly, in holding an enforced uniformity of religion in a civil state, we must necessarily disclaim our desires and hopes of the Jew's conversion to Christ.

Tenthly, an enforced uniformity of religion throughout a nation or civil state, confounds the civil and religious, denies the principles of Christianity and civility, and that Jesus Christ is come in the flesh.

Eleventhly, the permission of other consciences and worships than a state professeth only can (according to God) procure a firm and lasting peace (good assurance being taken according to the wisdom of the civil state for uniformity of civil obedience from all forts).

Twelfthly, lastly, true civility and Christianity may both flourish in a state or kingdom, notwithstanding the permission of diverse and contrary consciences, either of Jew or Gentile. . . .

Dialogue Between Truth and Peace

TRUTH. I acknowledge that to molest any person, Jew or Gentile, for either professing doctrine, or practicing worship merely religious or spiritual, it is to persecute him, and such a person (whatever his doctrine or practice be, true or false) suffereth persecution for conscience.

But withal I desire it may be well observed that this distinction is not full and complete: for beside this that a man may be persecuted because he holds or practices what he believes in conscience to be a truth (as [the biblical prophet] Daniel did, for which he was cast into the lions' den, Dan. 6), and many thousands of Christians, because they durst not cease to preach and practice what they believed was by God commanded, as the Apostles answered (Acts 4 & 5), I say besides this a man may also be persecuted, because he dares not be constrained to yield obedience to such doctrines and worships as are by men invented and appointed. . . .

PEACE. Dear TRUTH, I have two sad complaints:

First, the most sober of the witnesses, that dare to plead thy cause, how are they charged to be mine enemies, contentious, turbulent, seditious?

Secondly, thine enemies, though they speak and rail against thee, though they outrageously pursue, imprison, banish, kill thy faithful witnesses, yet how is all vermilion'd o'er [bloodied] for justice against the heretics? Yea, if they kindle coals, and blow the flames of devouring wars, that leave neither spiritual nor civil state, but burn up branch and root, yet how do all pretend an holy war? He that kills, and he that's killed, they both cry out: "It is for God, and for their conscience."

'Tis true, nor one nor other seldom dare to plead the mighty Prince Christ Jesus for their author, yet (both Protestant and Papist) pretend they have spoke with Moses and the Prophets who all, say they (before Christ came), allowed such holy persecutions, holy wars against the enemies of holy church.

Force Is Sometimes Necessary

TRUTH. Dear PEACE (to ease thy first complaint), 'tis true, thy dearest sons, most like their mother, peacekeeping, peacemaking sons of God, have borne and still must bear the blurs of troublers of Israel, and turners of the world upside down. And 'tis true again, what [Israelite king] Solomon once spake: "The beginning of strife is as when one letteth out water, therefore (saith he) leave off contention before it be meddled with. This caveat [warning] should keep the banks and sluices firm and strong, that strife, like a breach of waters, break not in upon the sons of men."

Yet strife must be distinguished: It is necessary or unnecessary, godly or Ungodly, Christian or unchristian, etc.

It is unnecessary, unlawful, dishonorable, ungodly, unchristian, in most cases in the world, for there is a possibility of keeping sweet peace in most cases, and, if it be possible, it is the express command of God that peace be kept (Rom. 13).

Again, it is necessary, honorable, godly, etc., with civil and earthly weapons to defend the innocent and to rescue the oppressed from the violent paws and jaws of oppressing persecuting Nimrods [tyrants] (Psal. 73; Job 29).

It is as necessary, yea more honorable, godly, and Christian, to fight the fight of faith, with religious and spiritual artillery, and to contend earnestly for the faith of Jesus, once delivered to the saints against all opposers, and the gates of earth and hell, men or devils, yea against Paul himself, or an angel from heaven, if he bring any other faith or doctrine. . . .

Force Does Not Win Converts

PEACE. I add that a civil sword (as woeful experience in all ages has proved) is so far from bringing or helping forward an opposite in religion to repentance that magistrates sin grievously against the work of God and blood of souls by such proceedings. Because as (commonly) the sufferings of false and antichristian teachers harden their followers, who being blind, by this means are occasioned to tumble into the ditch of hell after their blind leaders, with more inflamed zeal of lying confidence. So, secondly, violence and a sword of steel begets such an impression in the sufferers that certainly they conclude (as indeed that religion cannot be true which needs such instruments of violence to uphold it so) that persecutors are far from soft and gentle commiseration of the blindness of others. . . .

Government Must Outlaw False Doctrine

John Cotton

*Educated at Cambridge University, John Cotton was a promi-
nent theologian and preacher in England, but he was ultimately
forced to leave for his Nonconformist (those who disagreed with
the doctrines of the Church of England) views. He immigrated to
New England in 1633, where his views and his education were
highly prized. From the beginning he was a major influence in
both the religious and political life of the young colony. When a
Puritan nobleman named Lord Say and Seal thought of immi-
grating to the colony, he wrote to John Cotton for reassurance
about a particular point. He had heard that only church members could be citizens, regardless of their social standing, and he
feared that this might exclude him or his friends. John Cotton's
response is polite but firm, upholding the rule that only church
members could have a say in government. He admits that Christians can adapt to any government, and have no obligation to
change the political system in England. However, the unique case
of Massachusetts provides an opportunity to set up a government
that will more closely follow biblical ideals, he maintains. He
also rejects democracy as an ideal, arguing instead for a kind of
theocracy. The church would not directly decide issues, but magistrates and judges would be chosen from church members in
good standing. They in turn would have authority over church
members and nonmembers alike.*

It is very suitable to Gods all-sufficient wisdome, and to the
fulnes and perfection of Holy Scriptures, not only to prescribe perfect rules for the right ordering of a private mans

John Cotton, "A Letter from Mr. Cotton to Lord Say and Seal in the Year 1636," *The
Puritans: A Sourcebook of Their Writings: Two Volumes Bound in One.* Mineola, NY:
Dover Publications, 2001, pp. 209–212. Copyright © 2001 by Dover Publications, Inc.
Reproduced by permission.

soule to everlasting blessednes with himselfe, but also for the right ordering of a mans family, yea, of the commonwealth too, so farre as both of them are subordinate to spiritual ends, and yet avoide both the churches usurpation upon civill jurisdictions, ... and the commonwealths invasion upon ecclesiasticall administrations, ... to civill peace, and conformity to the civill state. Gods institutions (such as the government of church and of commonwealth be) may be close and compact, and co-ordinate one to another, and yet not confounded. God hath so framed the state of church government and ordinances, that they may be compatible to any common-wealth, though never so much disordered in his frame. But yet when a commonwealth hath liberty to mould his owne frame. ... I conceyve the scripture hath given full direction for the right ordering of the same, and that in such sort as may best mainteyne the *euexia* [vigor] of the church. Mr. [Thomas] Hooker doth often quote a saying out of Mr. [Thomas] Cartwright (though I have not read it in him) that noe man fashioneth his house to his hangings [furnishings], but his hangings to his house. It is better that the commonwealth be fashioned to the setting forth of Gods house, which is his church: than to accommodate the church frame to the civill state. Democracy, I do not conceyve that ever God did ordeyne as a fitt government weyther for church or commonwealth. If the people be governors, who shall be governed? As for monarchy, and aristocracy, they are both of them clearly approved, and directed in scripture, yet so as referreth the soveraigntie to himselfe, and setteth up Theocracy in both, as the best forme of government in the commonwealth, as well as in the church.

Magistrates Must Be Church Members

The law, which your Lordship instanceth [refers to] in (that none shall be chosen to magistracy among us but a church member) was made and enacted before I came into the country; but I have hitherto wanted [lacked] sufficient light to

plead against it. 1st. The rule that directeth the choice of supreme governors, is of like æquitie [equality] and wieht
[weight] in all magistrates, that one of their brethren (not a
stranger) should be set over them, Deut. 17.15, and Jethroes
counsell to Moses was approved of God, that the judges, and
officers to be set over the people, should be men fearing God,
Exod. 18. 21. and Solomon maketh it the joy of a commonwealth, when the righteous are in authority, and their mourn-
ing when the wicked rule, Prov. 29.21, Job 34.30, Your
Lordship's feare, that this will bring in papal excommunication, is just, and pious: but let your Lordship be pleased againe
to consider whether the consequence be necessary. *Turpius
ejicitur quam non admittitur*: [It is worse to be thrown out
than not admitted] non-membership may be a just cause of
non-admission to the place of magistracy. A godly woman, being to make choice of an husband, may justly refuse a man
that is eyther cast out of church fellowship, or is not yet re-
ceyved into it, but yet, when shee is once given to him, shee
may not reject him then, for such defect. . . .

Churches Will Not Govern Directly

When your Lordship doubteth, that this corse will draw all
things under the determination of the church, . . . (seeing the
church is to determine who shall be members, and none but a
member may have to doe in the government of a
commonwealth) be pleased (I pray you) to conceyve, that
magistrates are neyther chosen to office in the church, nor
doe governe by directions from the church, but by civill lawes,
and those enacted in generall corts, and executed in corts of
iustice, by the governors and assistants. In all which, the
church (as the church) hath nothing to doe: onely, it prep-
areth fitt instruments both to rule, and to choose rulers, which
is no ambition in the church, nor dishonor to the commonwealth, the apostle, on the contrary, thought it a great dishonor and reproach to the church of Christ, if it were not

able to yield able judges to heare and determine all causes amongst their brethren, I Cor. 6.1 to 5, which place alone seemeth to me fully to decide this question: for it plainely holdeth forth this argument: It is a shame to the church to want [lack] able judges of civill matters and an audacious act in any church member voluntarily to go for judgment, other-where than before the saints then it will be noe arrogance nor folly in church members, nor prejudice to the commonwealth, if voluntarily they never choose any civill judges, but from amongst the saints, such as church members are called to be. But the former is cleare: and how then can the latter be avoy-ded. If this therefore be (as your Lordship rightly conceyveth one of the maine objections if not the onely one) which hin-dereth this commonwealth from the entertainment of the propositions of those worthy gentlemen, wee intreate them, in the name of the Lord Jesus, to consider, in meeknes of wis-dome, it is not any conceite or will of ours, but the holy counsell and will of the Lord Jesus (whom they seeke to serve as well as wee) that overruleth us in this case: and we trust will overrule them also, that the Lord onely may be exalted amongst all his servants. What pittie and griefe were it, that the observance of the will of Christ should hinder good things from us!

An Opportunity for Christian Government

But your Lordship doubteth, that if such a rule were neces-sary, then the church estate and the best ordered common-wealth in the world were not compatible. But let not your Lordship so conceyve. For, the church submitteth itselfe to all the lawes and ordinances of men, in what commonwealth so-ever they come to dwell. But it is one thing, to submit unto what they have noe calling to reforme: another thing, volun-tarily to ordeyne a forme of government, which to the best discerning of many of us (for I speake not of myselfe) is ex-pressly contrary to rule. Nor neede your Lordship feare (which yet I speake with submission to your Lordships better judgment) that this corse will lay such a foundation as nothing but a mere democracy can be built upon it. [French political philosopher Jean] Bodine confesseth, that though it be *status popularis* [popular government], where a people choose their owne governors; yet the government is not a democracy, if it be administred, not by the people, but by the governors, whether one (for then it is a monarchy, though elective) or by many, for then (as you know) it is aristocracy. In which respect it is, that church government is iustly denyed to be democratical, though the people choose their owne officers and rulers.

Nor neede wee feare, that this course will, in time, cast the commonwealth into distractions, and popular confusions. For (under correction) these three things doe not undermine, but doe mutually and strongly mainteyne one another (even those three which wee principally aime at) authority in magistrates, liberty in people, purity in the church. Purity, preserved in the church, will preserve well ordered liberty in the people, and both of them establish well-ballanced authority in the magistrates. God is the author of all these three, and neyther is himselfe the God of confusion, nor are his wayes the wayes of confusion, but of peace. . . .

Government Should Be Mostly Neutral Regarding Religion

John Locke

It would be difficult to overestimate the influence of John Locke on the Founders. His theories of the state of nature and the social contract profoundly affected their views on government, law, economics, and philosophy in general. A key ingredient in his philosophy was tolerance, and in 1689 he set forth his ideas about religious tolerance. He draws a careful distinction between civil government and the role of religion, a revolutionary idea at the time. Rather than ensuring that people believed "correctly," he saw government's role as ensuring public order and public welfare, including people's natural rights to life and liberty. He argued that the use of force and the power of magistrates were entirely inappropriate in trying to save souls. For him, God did not approve of salvation through coercion, and persuasion was the only reasonable option. At the same time, he did set limits to tolerance. He opposed the toleration of Roman Catholicism, on the grounds that its own intolerance prevented it from coexisting peacefully in a tolerant society, and of atheism, on the grounds that atheists could not be trusted to keep oaths or other promises that bound society together. Born in 1632, Locke died in 1704.

Since you are pleased to inquire what are my thoughts about the mutual toleration of Christians in their different professions of religion, I must needs answer you freely that I esteem that toleration to be the chief characteristic mark of the true Church. For whatsoever some people boast of the antiquity of places and names, or of the pomp of their outward worship; others, of the reformation of their discipline; all, of the orthodoxy of their faith—for everyone is orthodox to himself—these things, and all others of this nature, are much

John Locke, "Letter Concerning Toleration," 1689. www.constitution.org.

rather marks of men striving for power and empire over one another than of the Church of Christ. Let anyone have never so true a claim to all these things, yet if he be destitute of charity, meekness, and good-will in general towards all mankind, even to those that are not Christians, he is certainly yet short of being a true Christian himself. "The kings of the Gentiles exercise leadership over them," said our Saviour to his disciples, "but ye shall not be so." [Luke 22:25] The business of true religion is quite another thing. It is not instituted in order to the erecting of an external pomp, nor to the obtaining of ecclesiastical dominion, nor to the exercising of compulsive force, but to the regulating of men's lives, according to the rules of virtue and piety. Whosoever will list himself under the banner of Christ, must, in the first place and above all things, make war upon his own lusts and vices. It is in vain for any man to usurp the name of Christian, without holiness of life, purity of manners, benignity and meekness of spirit. "Let everyone that nameth the name of Christ, depart from iniquity." [2 Tim 2:19] "Thou, when thou art converted, strengthen thy brethren," said our Lord to Peter. [Luke 22:32] It would, indeed, be very hard for one that appears careless about his own salvation to persuade me that he were extremely concerned for mine. For it is impossible that those should sincerely and heartily apply themselves to make other people Christians, who have not really embraced the Christian religion in their own hearts. If the Gospel and the apostles may be credited, no man can be a Christian without charity and without that faith which works, not by force, but by love. Now, I appeal to the consciences of those that persecute, torment, destroy, and kill other men upon pretence of religion, whether they do it out of friendship and kindness towards them or no. And I shall then indeed, and not until then, believe they do so, when I shall see those fiery zealots correcting, in the same manner, their friends and familiar acquaintance for the manifest sins they commit against the precepts of the

Gospel; when I shall see them persecute with fire and sword the members of their own communion that are tainted with enormous vices and without amendment are in danger of eternal perdition; and when I shall see them thus express their love and desire of the salvation of their souls by the infliction of torments and exercise of all manner of cruelties. For if it be out of a principle of charity, as they pretend, and love to men's souls that they deprive them of their estates, maim them with corporal punishments, starve and torment them in noisome prisons, and in the end even take away their lives—I say, if all this be done merely to make men Christians and procure their salvation, why then do they suffer whoredom, fraud, malice, and such-like enormities, which (according to the apostle) [Rom. 1] manifestly relish of heathenish corruption, to predominate so much and abound amongst their flocks and people? These, and such-like things, are certainly more contrary to the glory of God, to the purity of the Church, and to the salvation of souls, than any conscientious dissent from ecclesiastical [official church] decisions, or separation from public worship, whilst accompanied with innocence of life. Why, then, does this burning zeal for God, for the Church, and for the salvation of souls—burning I say, literally, with fire and faggot [firewood]—pass by those moral vices and wickednesses, without any chastisement, which are acknowledged by all men to be diametrically opposite to the profession of Christianity, and bend all its nerves either to the introducing of ceremonies, or to the establishment of opinions, which for the most part are about nice [precise] and intricate matters, that exceed the capacity of ordinary understandings? Which of the parties contending about these things is in the right, which of them is guilty of schism or heresy, whether those that domineer or those that suffer, will then at last be manifest when the causes of their separation comes to be judged of He, certainly, that follows Christ, embraces His doctrine, and bears His yoke, though he forsake both father and mother, separate from the public assemblies and ceremonies of his country, or whomsoever or whatsoever else he relinquishes, will not then be judged a heretic.

Sin Persists in All Religions

Now, though the divisions that are amongst sects should be allowed to be never so obstructive of the salvation of souls; yet, nevertheless, adultery, fornication, uncleanliness, lasciviousness, idolatry, and such-like things, cannot be denied to be works of the flesh, concerning which the apostle has expressly declared that "they who do them shall not inherit the kingdom of God." [Gal. 5] Whosoever, therefore, is sincerely solicitous about the kingdom of God and thinks it his duty to endeavour the enlargement of it amongst men, ought to apply himself with no less care and industry to the rooting out of these immoralities than to the extirpation of sects. But if anyone do otherwise, and whilst he is cruel and implacable towards those that differ from him in opinion, he be indulgent to such iniquities and immoralities as are unbecoming the name of a Christian, let such a one talk never so much of the Church, he plainly demonstrates by his actions that it is another kingdom he aims at and not the advancement of the kingdom of God.

That any man should think fit to cause another man—whose salvation he heartily desires—to expire in torments, and that even in an unconverted state, would, I confess, seem very strange to me, and I think, to any other also. But nobody, surely, will ever believe that such a carriage [attitude] can proceed from charity, love, or goodwill. If anyone maintain that men ought to be compelled by fire and sword to profess certain doctrines, and conform to this or that exterior worship, without any regard had unto their morals; if anyone endeavour to convert those that are erroneous unto the faith, by forcing them to profess things that they do not believe and allowing them to practise things that the Gospel does not permit, it cannot be doubted indeed but such a one is desirous to have a numerous assembly joined in the same profession with himself; but that he principally intends by those means to compose a truly Christian Church is altogether incredible. It is not, therefore, to be wondered at if those who do not really contend for the advancement of the true religion, and of the Church of Christ, make use of arms that do not belong to the Christian warfare. If, like the Captain of our salvation, they sincerely desired the good of souls, they would tread in the steps and follow the perfect example of that Prince of Peace, who sent out His soldiers to the subduing of nations, and gathering them into His Church, not armed with the sword, or other instruments of force, but prepared with the Gospel of peace and with the exemplary holiness of their conversation. This was His method. Though if infidels [unbelievers] were to be converted by force, if those that are either blind or obstinate were to be drawn off from their errors by armed soldiers, we know very well that it was much more easy for Him to do it with armies of heavenly legions than for any son of the Church, how potent [powerful] soever, with all his dragoons [soldiers].

The toleration of those that differ from others in matters of religion is so agreeable to the Gospel of Jesus Christ, and to the genuine reason of mankind, that it seems monstrous for men to be so blind as not to perceive the necessity and advantage of it in so clear a light. I will not here tax the pride and ambition of some, the passion and uncharitable zeal of others. These are faults from which human affairs can perhaps scarce ever be perfectly freed; but yet such as nobody will bear the plain imputation of, without covering them with some specious colour; and so pretend to commendation, whilst they are carried away by their own irregular passions. But, however, that some may not colour their spirit of persecution and unchristian cruelty with a pretence of care of the public weal [welfare] and observation of the laws; and that others, under pretence of religion, may not seek impunity for their libertinism and licentiousness; in a word, that none may impose either upon himself or others, by the pretences of loyalty and obedience to the prince, or of tenderness and sincerity in the worship of God; I esteem it above all things necessary to distinguish exactly the business of civil government from that of religion and to settle the just bounds that lie between the one and the other. If this be not done, there can be no end put to the controversies that will be always arising between those that have, or at least pretend to have, on the one side, a concernment for the interest of men's souls, and, on the other side, a care of the commonwealth.

The commonwealth seems to me to be a society of men constituted only for the procuring, preserving, and advancing their own civil interests.

Civil Interests

Civil interests I call life, liberty, health, and indolency of body; and the possession of outward things, such as money, lands, houses, furniture, and the like.

It is the duty of the civil magistrate, by the impartial execution of equal laws, to secure unto all the people in general and to every one of his subjects in particular the just possession of these things belonging to this life. If anyone presume to violate the laws of public justice and equity, established for the preservation of those things, his presumption is to be checked by the fear of punishment, consisting of the deprivation or diminution of those civil interests, or goods, which otherwise he might and ought to enjoy. But seeing no man does willingly suffer himself to be punished by the deprivation of any part of his goods, and much less of his liberty or life, therefore, is the magistrate armed with the force and strength of all his subjects, in order to the punishment of those that violate any other man's rights.

Now that the whole jurisdiction of the magistrate reaches only to these civil concernments, and that all civil power, right and dominion, is bounded and confined to the only care of promoting these things; and that it neither can nor ought in any manner to be extended to the salvation of souls, these following considerations seem unto me abundantly to demonstrate.

First, because the care of souls is not committed to the civil magistrate, any more than to other men. It is not committed unto him, I say, by God; because it appears not that God has ever given any such authority to one man over another as to compel anyone to his religion. Nor can any such power be vested in the magistrate by the consent of the people, because no man can so far abandon the care of his own salvation as blindly to leave to the choice of any other, whether prince or subject, to prescribe to him what faith or worship he shall embrace. For no man can, if he would, conform his faith to the dictates of another. All the life and power of true religion consist in the inward and full persuasion of the mind; and faith is not faith without believing. Whatever profession we make, to whatever outward worship we conform, if we are not fully satisfied in our own mind that the one is true and the other well pleasing unto God, such profession and such practice, far from being any furtherance, are indeed great obstacles to our salvation. For in this manner, instead of expiating other sins by the exercise of religion, I say, in offering thus unto God Almighty such a worship as we esteem to be displeasing unto Him, we add unto the number of our other sins those also of hypocrisy and contempt of His Divine Majesty.

In the second place, the care of souls cannot belong to the civil magistrate, because his power consists only in outward force; but true and saving religion consists in the inward persuasion of the mind, without which nothing can be acceptable to God. And such is the nature of the understanding, that it cannot be compelled to the belief of anything by outward force. Confiscation of estate, imprisonment, torments, nothing of that nature can have any such efficacy as to make men change the inward judgement that they have framed of things.

It may indeed be alleged that the magistrate may make use of arguments, and, thereby; draw the heterodox [dissenters] into the way of truth, and procure their salvation. I grant it; but this is common to him with other men. In teaching, instructing, and redressing the erroneous by reason, he may certainly do what becomes any good man to do. Magistracy does not oblige him to put off either humanity or Christianity; but it is one thing to persuade, another to command; one thing to press with arguments, another with penalties. This civil power alone has a right to do; to the other, goodwill is authority enough. Every man has commission to admonish, exhort, convince another of error, and, by reasoning, to draw him into truth; but to give laws, receive obedience, and compel with the sword, belongs to none but the magistrate. And, upon this ground, I affirm that the magistrate's power extends not to the establishing of any articles of faith, or forms of worship, by the force of his laws. For laws are of no force at all without penalties, and penalties in this case are absolutely impertinent, because they are not proper to convince the mind. Neither the profession of any articles of faith, nor the conformity to any outward form of worship (as has been already said), can be available to the salvation of souls, unless the truth of the one and the acceptableness of the other unto God be thoroughly believed by those that so profess and practise. But penalties are no way capable to produce such belief. It is only light and evidence that can work a change in men's opinions; which light can in no manner proceed from corporal sufferings, or any other outward penalties.

In the third place, the care of the salvation of men's souls cannot belong to the magistrate; because, though the rigour of laws and the force of penalties were capable to convince and change men's minds, yet would not that help at all to the salvation of their souls. For there being but one truth, one way to heaven, what hope is there that more men would be led into it if they had no rule but the religion of the court and were put under the necessity to quit the light of their own reason, and oppose the dictates of their own consciences, and blindly to resign themselves up to the will of their governors and to the religion which either ignorance, ambition, or superstition had chanced to establish in the countries where they were born? In the variety and contradiction of opinions in religion, wherein the princes of the world are as much divided as in their secular interests, the narrow way would be much straitened [constricted]; one country alone would be in the right, and all the rest of the world put under an obligation of following their princes in the ways that lead to destruction; and that which heightens the absurdity, and very ill suits the notion of a Deity, men would owe their eternal happiness or misery to the places of their nativity.

These considerations, to omit many others that might have been urged to the same purpose, seem unto me sufficient to conclude that all the power of civil government relates only to men's civil interests, is confined to the care of the things of this world, and hath nothing to do with the world to come.

Church Membership Is Voluntary

Let us now consider what a church is. A church, then, I take to be a voluntary society of men, joining themselves together of their own accord in order to the public worshipping of God in such manner as they judge acceptable to Him, and effectual to the salvation of their souls.

I say it is a free and voluntary society. Nobody is born a member of any church; otherwise the religion of parents would descend unto children by the same right of inheritance as their temporal estates, and everyone would hold his faith by the same tenure he does his lands, than which nothing can be imagined more absurd. Thus, therefore, that matter stands.

No man by nature is bound unto any particular church or sect, but everyone joins himself voluntarily to that society in which he believes he has found that profession and worship which is truly acceptable to God. The hope of salvation, as it was the only cause of his entrance into that communion, so it can be the only reason of his stay there. For if afterwards he discover anything either erroneous in the doctrine or incongruous in the worship of that society to which he has joined himself, why should it not be as free for him to go out as it was to enter? No member of a religious society can be tied with any other bonds but what proceed from the certain expectation of eternal life. A church, then, is a society of members voluntarily uniting to that end. . . .

Exceptions

But to come to particulars. I say, first, no opinions contrary to human society, or to those moral rules which are necessary to the preservation of civil society, are to be tolerated by the magistrate. But of these, indeed, examples in any Church are rare. For no sect can easily arrive to such a degree of madness as that it should think fit to teach, for doctrines of religion, such things as manifestly undermine the foundations of society and are, therefore, condemned by the judgement of all mankind; because their own interest, peace, reputation, everything would be thereby endangered.

Another more secret evil, but more dangerous to the commonwealth, is when men arrogate to themselves, and to those of their own sect, some peculiar prerogative covered over with a specious show of deceitful words, but in effect opposite to the civil right of the community. For example: we cannot find any sect that teaches, expressly and openly, that men are not obliged to keep their promise; that princes may be dethroned by those that differ from them in religion; or that the dominion of all things belongs only to themselves. For these things, proposed thus nakedly and plainly, would soon draw on them the eye and hand of the magistrate and awaken all the care of the commonwealth to a watchfulness against the spreading of so dangerous an evil. But, nevertheless, we find those that say the same things in other words. What else do they mean who teach that faith is not to be kept with heretics? Their meaning, forsooth [indeed], is that the privilege of breaking faith belongs unto themselves; for they declare all that are not of their communion to be heretics, or at least may declare them so whensoever they think fit. What can be the meaning of their asserting that kings excommunicated forfeit their crowns and kingdoms? It is evident that they thereby arrogate unto themselves the power of deposing kings, because they challenge the power of excommunication, as the peculiar right of their hierarchy. That dominion is founded in grace is also an assertion by which those that maintain it do plainly lay claim to the possession of all things. For they are not so wanting to themselves as not to believe, or at least as not to profess themselves to be the truly pious and faithful. These, therefore, and the like, who attribute unto the faithful, religious, and orthodox, that is, in plain terms, unto themselves, any peculiar privilege or power above other mortals, in civil concernments; or who upon pretence of religion do challenge any manner of authority over such as are not associated with them in their ecclesiastical communion, I say these have no right to be tolerated by the magistrate; as neither those that will not own and teach the duty of tolerating all men in matters of mere religion. For what do all these and the like doctrines signify, but that they may and are ready upon any occasion to seize the Government and possess themselves of the estates and fortunes of their fellow subjects; and that they only ask leave to be tolerated by the magistrate so long until they find themselves strong enough to effect it?

Again: That Church can have no right to be tolerated by the magistrate which is constituted upon such a bottom [foundation] that all those who enter into it do thereby ipso facto [by that fact itself] deliver themselves up to the protection and service of another prince. For by this means the magistrate would give way to the settling of a foreign jurisdiction in his own country and suffer his own people to be listed, as it were, for soldiers against his own Government. Nor does the frivolous and fallacious distinction between the Court and the Church afford any remedy to this inconvenience; especially when both the one and the other are equally subject to the absolute authority of the same person, who has not only power to persuade the members of his Church to whatsoever he lists, either as purely religious, or in order thereunto, but can also enjoin it them on pain of eternal fire. It is ridiculous for any one to profess himself to be a Mahometan [Muslim] only in his religion, but in everything else a faithful subject to a Christian magistrate, whilst at the same time he acknowledges himself bound to yield blind obedience to the Mufti of Constantinople, who himself is entirely obedient to the Ottoman Emperor and frames the feigned oracles of that religion according to his pleasure. But this Mahometan living amongst Christians would yet more apparently renounce their government if he acknowledged the same person to be head of his Church who is the supreme magistrate in the state.

Lastly, those are not at all to be tolerated who deny the being of a God. Promises, covenants, and oaths, which are the bonds of human society, can have no hold upon an atheist. The taking away of God, though but even in thought, dissolves all; besides also, those that by their atheism undermine and destroy all religion, can have no pretence of religion whereupon to challenge the privilege of a toleration. As for other practical opinions, though not absolutely free from all error, if they do not tend to establish domination over others, or civil impunity to the Church in which they are taught, there can be no reason why they should not be tolerated.

CHAPTER 2

Church and State in the New Republic

Chapter Preface

It is easy to make two big mistakes about the religion of the Founders. The first is to declare that they were all Deists; that is, that they saw God as setting the world in motion through natural laws and then leaving it alone. The second is to declare that this is a Christian nation founded on a Constitution based on Judeo-Christian ideals. Still, there is just enough truth in both ideas to keep them coming back.

It is true that the latter half of the eighteenth century, the Age of Enlightenment, saw a vigorous attack on traditional religious institutions, which were accused of promoting warfare, superstition, cruelty, and despotism. The religious wars of the sixteenth and seventeenth century, especially the savage Thirty Years War in which Catholics and Protestants decimated Germany, led to a profound disgust with religion's stranglehold on politics and science. Philosophers like David Hume in England and Voltaire in France insisted that religious claims had to be tested like everything else, and tossed out if they were proven false. Thomas Jefferson, who was a Deist, eagerly embraced this idea and sought to create a society in which no church could force its doctrines on anyone, where all would be completely free to believe or not believe any religious idea. This idea, of course, is incorporated in the First Amendment to the U.S. Constitution and, in the body of the Constitution itself, the statement that no religious test can be applied to anyone seeking government office.

At the same time, a different kind of disgust had created a dramatic change in America's religious landscape. The fervor of the original Puritan settlers of New England had decreased with each new generation. Then, in the 1730s and 1740s, the old Puritan spirit seemed to come alive again, particular in the sermons of John Edwards. Edwards demanded a deeply personal, emotional devotion to a God whose love was the only thing that could save them from the horrors of hell. At the same time, Methodist preacher George Whitefield was attracting huge crowds to his revivals in the villages and small towns of the middle and southern states. The result was an expansion of smaller sects, such as the Baptists, Methodists, and Presbyterians, who deeply resented having to support the established Anglican and Congregationalist churches. This so-called Great Awakening would play a role in creating the Establishment Clause of the First Amendment.

Both contemporary visitors and modern historians have noted the combination of skepticism and religious fervor of this period in America. Jefferson and James Madison certainly succeeded in breaking the official ties between church and state, both in the federal government and their own state of Virginia. For the first time, citizens were free to reject, ignore, or attack religious institutions without facing criminal or civil prosecution. Many of those citizens, however, embraced this freedom by flocking to churches that put religious belief even more squarely at the center of their lives. This contrast between a secular, religiously neutral Constitution and the emotional power of religion and churches over so many Americans has been a puzzle and a challenge to quite a few historians and politicians over the last two centuries.

Baptists Call for Freedom from Supporting Other Religions

William G. McLoughlin

The American Revolution created an opportunity for Baptists in Massachusetts, who had long resented having to pay for the support of the established Congregationalist Church. Eventually, the Massachusetts delegates to the Continental Congress, including John and Samuel Adams, agreed to meet with Isaac Backus, a leading Baptist preacher, along with a number of other officials and a group of Quaker leaders. At the meeting, which took place in Philadelphia, Backus presented a memorial stating the Baptists' grievances and calling upon the new Congress to support them. The Massachusetts delegates dismissed complaints of general persecution and called upon the Baptists to submit individual complaints to the local courts and legislature. The presence of the Quakers, led by Israel Pemberton, also caused problems, as they were suspected of loyalist sympathies. John Adams saw the entire incident as little more than an attempt to cause disunity in the colonies, and delegate R.T. Paine explicitly made this charge back in Massachusetts. In the end, the provincial Congress of Massachusetts accepted a petition from Backus, but they did little more than give a polite reply. Ultimately, of course, the determination of people like Isaac Backus to eliminate established churches would prevail, but the incident does illustrate the more complicated feelings of the Founding generation.

William G. McLoughlin was a professor of history at Brown University from 1954 until his death in 1992. He is the author

William G. McLoughlin, "Civil Disobedience and the Appeal to Congress, 1773–1774," *New England Dissent, 1630–1833: The Baptists and the Separation of Church and State*, Cambridge, MA: Harvard University Press, 1971, pp. 559–565. Copyright © 1971 by the President and Fellows of Harvard College. All rights reserved. Reproduced by permission of Harvard University Press.

of eighteen books on the history of religion and other aspects of American history, including major works on the history of the Cherokee Nation.

A meeting was arranged for Friday night, October 14, [1774,] in Carpenters' Hall. The four Massachusetts delegates were invited (John Adams, Samuel Adams, Robert Treat Paine, and Thomas Cushing) as were . . . the three Quaker leaders; a number of Baptists who were members of the Philadelphia Association and the New England Baptists. Others, whose names are unknown, were also present. [Isaac] Backus and Robert Strettle Jones had prepared for the occasion a memorial which James Manning read to open the discussion.

The memorial is not a very striking document. It contained a mixture of pietistic arguments, political theory, and legalistic interpretations of the charter and ecclesiastical laws of Massachusetts. It summarized the tax exemption acts and described some of the oppressions committed under them (especially those in Sturbridge and Ashfield). It concluded with a quotation from "the great Mr. Locke" intended to prove that the magistrates's power did not extend to spiritual affairs, thus supporting the argument that the Baptists were in effect being taxed without representation by being forced to support a religious system which was established by civil power and which they could not in conscience adhere to. It concluded,

> It may now be asked—What is the liberty desired? The answer is; as the kingdom of Christ is not of this world and religion is a concern between God and the soul with which no human authority can intermeddle . . . we claim and expect the liberty of worshipping God according to our consciences, not being obliged to support a ministry we cannot attend, whilst we demean ourselves as faithful subjects.

In response to this "John Adams made a long speech, and Samuel Adams another, both of whom said, 'There is indeed an ecclesiastical establishment in our province; but a very slender one, hardly to be called an establishment.'" The Baptists tried to insist that it was a very rigid and oppressive establishment and cited cases of persecution. Then the Massachusetts delegates "shifted their plea, and asserted that our General Court was clear of blame, and had always been ready to hear our complaints, and to grant all reasonable help, whatever might have been done by [local] executive officers; and S. Adams and R. T. Paine spent near an hour more on this plea." Backus then presented to them the history of the Ashfield law "which was very puzzling to them." Paine throughout the discussion "insinuated that these complaints came from enthusiasts [fanatics] who made it a merit to suffer persecution" and implied that enemies of the colony were at work in this (presumably a reference to Thomas Hutchinson's assistance to the Baptists in the Ashfield case). Paine also insisted that the Baptists' refusal since 1773 to give in certificates was largely to blame; according to Paine this refusal meant, said Backus, "that we would not be neighborly and let them know who we were, which was all they wanted, and they would readily exempt us." At bottom, Paine concluded, "There was nothing of conscience in the matter; it was only a contending about paying a little money."

At this insinuation Backus retorted that no matter what it was to Paine, "It is absolutely a point of conscience with me; for I cannot give in the certificates they require without implicitly acknowledging that power in man which I believe belongs to God." At last he seemed to have made an impression. "This shocked them, and Cushing said: 'It quite altered the case; for if it were a point of conscience, he had nothing to say to that.'" The conference ended with "their promising to do what they could for our relief."

But Backus and his friends refused to take much stock in this, for during the course of the debate both John Adams and R. T. Paine had expressed complete opposition to giving up their establishment. According to Backus, Adams at one point

told the Baptists "We might as soon expect a change in the so-
lar system, as to expect they would give up their establishment;" at another time he and Paine said "We might as soon
expect that they would submit to the Port Bill, to the Regulating bill, and the Murder bill as to give up that establishment."
Yet, commented Backus, Adams and Paine "in the beginning
of their pleas called [their establishment] a very slender thing.
Such absurdities does religious tyranny produce in great men."

This of course is the debate as the Baptists saw and related
it. . . .

Role of the Quakers

The part of the story that the Baptists did not tell, perhaps
did not realize, was the role of the Quakers. In none of their
accounts is it evident that the Quakers spoke at all during the
meeting. Yet when one reads the accounts written by the Massachusetts delegates themselves, it is plain that it was what the
Quakers said and did at this meeting which made the greatest
impression upon them. According to both Adams and Paine,
Israel Pemberton launched a great deal of bitter invective
against Massachusetts for its intolerance and asserted that it
was up to Massachusetts to bring its religious laws in har-
mony with the rest of the colonies. Since the Quakers, led by
Pemberton, were well-known to be neutral if not loyalist at
this time and even later; and since even many Baptists—like
Morgan Edwards—in the Middle Colonies were suspected of
loyalist leanings, it is not surprising that Adams and Paine
looked upon the whole affair as an attempt to disrupt colonial
unity and to break up the Continental Congress by introducing extraneous and contentious issues. . . .

Meeting Causes Consternation

John Adams' account of the Philadelphia meeting reflects the
same consternation as does Paine's. He was, he wrote, "greatly
surprised and somewhat indignant" when he arrived at

Carpenter's Hall to find "our State and the delegates thus summoned before a self-created tribunal which was neither legal nor constitutional." Like Paine he placed much of the blame for the affair upon Israel Pemberton, "A Quaker of large property and more intrigue" who said that the unity of the colonies depended upon "engaging us to assure them that our State would repeal all those [ecclesiastical laws] and place things as they were in Pennsylvania." Adams was convinced that Pemberton "was endeavoring to avail himself of this opportunity to break up the Congress." Adams told Pemberton "That the people of Massachusetts were as religious and conscientious as the people of Pennsylvania; that their conscience dictated to them that it was their duty to support those laws, and therefore the very liberty of conscience, which Mr. Pemberton invoked, would demand indulgence for the tender consciences of the people of Massachusetts, and allow them to preserve their laws." To which, Adams wrote, "Pemberton made no reply but this: 'Oh! sir, pray don't urge liberty of conscience in favor of such laws!'" Adams was convinced that he and his friends had adequately defended themselves against their accusers: "Mr. Paine and I had been concerned at the bar in every action in the executive courts which was complained of, and we explained them all to the entire satisfaction of impartial men, and showed that there had been no oppression or injustice in any of them." Still Adams and the others promised "to do what they could" to correct any injustices in the application of the ecclesiastical laws.

Charge of Disloyalty

Backus returned to Middleborough on November 19, 1774, where he found that R.T. Paine, who had preceded him, had spread the view that the Baptists and Quakers had been employed in Philadelphia by enemies of the American cause to divide the country in its time of danger. He found also that his neighbors in Middleborough had voted to assess ministerial rates upon the members of his congregation because they refused to give in certificates. Backus called a meeting of the Grievance Committee on December 2 and with their approval sent a long petition to the Massachusetts Provincial Congress meeting at Cambridge. He protested that the Baptists were not enemies to the patriots' cause and he asked once again that the tax exemption law be revised. This petition was notable mainly for its extended attempt to argue that the Baptists, in fighting for religious liberty, were fighting for the same principles the patriots were fighting for against Parliament: "Not to be taxed where they are not represented and—To have their cause tried by unbiased judges." The requirement that Baptists pay four pence to obtain a copy of their certificates he compared to the Stamp Tax on tea:

> Great complaints have been made about a tax which the British Parliament laid upon paper; but you require a paper tax of us annually. That which has made the greatest noise is a tax of three pence upon tea; but your law of last June laid a tax of the same sum every year upon the Baptists in each parish, as they would expect to defend themselves against a greater one. (Apparently Backus believed that all Baptists would want or need a copy of their certificates annually so that they would have to pay four pence to get them.) "All America are alarmed at the tea tax; though if they please, they can avoid it by not buying the tea; but we have no such liberty. We must either pay the little tax, or else your people appear even in this time of extremity to lay the great one [ministerial rates] upon us." As Backus saw it, the assessors would always ignore certificates filed with the town clerk, and the individual would have to have his own copy in hand in order to withstand the tax collector. He made a summary of the recent cases of oppression in Montague, Chelmsford, Haverhill, Scarborough, Ashfield, Warwick, and now Middleborough, and maintained again "We cannot give the certificates you require without implicitly allowing to man that authority which we believe in our consciences be-

longs only to God. Here, therefore, we claim charter rights, liberty of conscience." In conclusion, having explained that his errand to Philadelphia was only to ask the aid of Congress in seeking "the future welfare of our country," he said, "We remain hearty friends to our country and ready to do all in our power for its general welfare."

When John Hancock asked the Provincial Congress whether they wished to hear Backus's petition the Congregationalists said no, but other deputies, some of them Baptists, called for its reading. The Congress seemed unwilling to take any action upon it until John Adams rose and, according to Hezekiah Smith, "said he was apprehensive if they threw it out it might cause a division among the provinces and it was his advice to do something about it." To this extent Backus's trip to Philadelphia was successful. But all the Provincial Congress did was to appoint a committee which declared that the Baptists should apply to the General Court and not to them. A tactfully worded resolution was sent to Backus saying that the Congress sincerely wanted "civil and religious liberty to each denomination in this province," but that they had no power to take any action in the matter and suggested that if the Baptists would lay their grievances before the next General Assembly they "will most certainly meet with all that attention due to the memorial of a denomination of Christians so well disposed to the public weal of their country."

Government Does Not Need an Established Religion

Thomas Jefferson and James Madison

State religions had been replaced by other state religions through-out history, as when the Roman Empire turned from paganism to Christianity, or when England switched from Catholicism to Anglicanism. The Virginia statute was the first, however, to de-clare that a government could get along without any established religion at all. The first section argues that forcing any doctrines onto citizens is wrong, an affront to both reason and to God, and that civil rights do not depend on religious beliefs. The next section forbids requiring anyone to support any religion or to at-tend any religious service. The last section declares this a natural right of all mankind, almost forbidding future assemblies to overturn the law.

Thomas Jefferson and James Madison, the third and fourth presidents of the United States, respectively, were two of the most influential Founders. Jefferson was the author of the Declaration of Independence, the head of the "Jeffersonian" faction that grew into the Democratic Party, and a tireless advocate for small gov-ernment and the use of reason rather than coercion. He is also the original source of the phrase "wall of separation" between church and state, which appears in one of his letters. Jefferson had the Virginia statute listed on his tombstone as one of his three most important accomplishments. Madison, the "Father of the Constitution," was the author of many of the Federalist Pa-pers that continue to influence constitutional interpretation and political theories to this day.

[Sec. 1] Whereas Almighty God hath created the mind free; that all attempts to influence it by temporal pun-ishments or burthens [burdens], or by civil incapacitations,

Thomas Jefferson and James Madison, "Virginia Statute for Religious Freedom," 1786.
http://usinfo.state.gove/infousa/government/overview/42.html.

tend only to beget habits of hypocrisy and meanness, and are a departure from the plan of the Holy author of our religion, who being Lord, both of body and mind, yet chose not to propagate it by coercions on either, as was in his Almighty power to do; that the impious presumption of legislators and rulers, civil as well as ecclesiastical, who being themselves but fallible and uninspired men, have assumed dominion over the faith of others, setting up their own opinions and modes of thinking as the only true and infallible, and as such endeavouring to impose them on others, hath established and maintained false religions over the greatest part of the world, and through all time; that to compel a man to furnish contributions of money for the propagation of opinions which he disbelieves, is sinful and tyrannical; that even the forcing him to support this or that teacher of his own religious persuasion, is depriving him of the comfortable liberty of giving his contributions to the particular pastor, whose morals he would make his pattern, and whose powers he feels most persuasive to righteousness, and is withdrawing from the ministry those temporary rewards, which proceeding from an approbation of their personal conduct, are an additional incitement to earnest and unremitting labours for the instruction of mankind; that our civil rights have no dependence on our religious opinions, any more than our opinions in physics or geometry; that therefore the proscribing [of] any citizen as unworthy the public confidence by laying upon him an incapacity of being called to offices of trust and emolument, unless he profess or renounce this or that religious opinion, is depriving him injuriously of those privileges and advantages to which in common with his fellow-citizens, he has a natural right; that it tends only to corrupt the principles of that religion it is meant to encourage, by bribing with a monopoly of worldly honours and emoluments, those who will externally profess and conform to it; that though indeed, these are criminal who do not withstand such temptation, yet neither are those innocent who lay the bait in their way; that to suffer the civil magistrate to intrude his powers into the field of opinion, and to restrain the profession or propagation of principles on supposition of their ill tendency, is a dangerous fallacy, which at once destroys all religious liberty, because he being of course judge of that tendency will make his opinions the rule of judgment, and approve or condemn the sentiments of others only as they shall square with or differ from his own; that it is time enough for the rightful purposes of civil government, for its officers to interfere when principles break out into overt acts against peace and good order; and finally, that truth is great and will prevail if left to herself, that she is the proper and sufficient antagonist to error, and has nothing to fear from the conflict, unless by human interposition disarmed of her natural weapons, free argument and debate, errors ceasing to be dangerous when it is permitted freely to contradict them:

No Religious Compulsion

[Sec. 2] Be it enacted by General Assembly, That no man shall be compelled to frequent or support any religious worship, place, or ministry whatsoever, nor shall be enforced, restrained, molested, or burthened in his body or goods, nor shall otherwise suffer on account of his religious opinions or belief; but that all men shall be free to profess, and by argument to maintain, their opinion in matters of religion, and that the same shall in no wise diminish, enlarge, or affect their civil capacities.

[Sec. 3] And though we well know that this assembly elected by the people for the ordinary purposes of legislation only, have no power to restrain the acts of succeeding assemblies, constituted with powers equal to our own, and that therefore to declare this act irrevocable would be of no effect in law; yet we are free to declare, and do declare, that the rights hereby asserted, are of the natural rights of mankind, and that if any act shall be hereafter passed to repeal the present, or to narrow its operation, such act will be an infringement of natural right.

Strong Religious Feelings Persist After the American Revolution

Gordon S. Wood

The eighteenth century, at least among the elite, was remarkably nonreligious. As Gordon S. Wood explains in the following excerpt, even the conservative Alexander Hamilton, when asked why God had been left out of the Constitution, responded, "We forgot." In the nineteenth century, it's unlikely any politician would make such a joke. Instead the country went through a religious revival called the Second Great Awakening, during which many people embraced both personal salvation and social reform. While some denounced this revival of "superstition," others embraced it as a means of uniting people in a society that was becoming too individualistic in so many ways. In fact, the record on this was mixed. Old, established churches found themselves competing with newer, rapidly growing, evangelical denominations. Religion became more personal than ever before and thus more fragmented. At the same time, highly influential members of the clergy began to take a much more serious interest in reshaping society, now that their congregations were the ultimate governors. Throughout the country, "moral societies" sprang up to fight against immoral "licentiousness" in the battle for public opinion.

Born in 1933, Gordon S. Wood is a professor of history at Brown University. In 1993, he won the Pulitzer Prize for History for the book from which this excerpt was taken.

Gordon S. Wood, "The Celebration of Commerce," *The Radicalism of the American Revolution*, New York: Vintage, 1992, pp. 330–334. Copyright © 1992 by Gordon S. Wood. All rights reserved. Used by permission of Alfred A. Knoft, a division of Random House, Inc.

At the time of the Revolution most of the founding fathers had not put much emotional stock in religion, even when they were regular churchgoers. . . . At best, most of the revolutionary gentry only passively believed in organized Christianity and, at worst, privately scorned and ridiculed it. [Thomas] Jefferson hated orthodox clergymen, and he repeatedly denounced the "priestcraft" for having converted Christianity into "an engine for enslaving mankind, . . . into a mere contrivance to filch wealth and power to themselves." Although few of them were outright deists, most, like David Ramsay, described the Christian church as "the best example of reason." Even puritanical John Adams thought that the argument for Christ's divinity was an "awful blasphemy" in this new enlightened age. When [Alexander] Hamilton was asked why the members of the Philadelphia Convention had not recognized God in the Constitution, he allegedly replied, speaking for many of his liberal colleagues, "We forgot."

By the early decades of the nineteenth century it was no longer so easy for enlightened gentlemen to forget God. If the democratic revolution of the decades following the Declaration of Independence meant the rise of ordinary people, it meant as well the rise of popular evangelical Christianity; for religion was the way most common people still made meaningful the world around them. By the early 1800s these common people were asserting their evangelical Christianity in ways that gentry leaders could no longer ignore. When Aaron Burr, grandson of [famous preacher] Jonathan Edwards, was criticized in 1801 for his neglect of religion, a close political associate reminded him of the Presbyterian vote and warned: "Had you not better go to church?" Even Hamilton in despair sought to wrap the mantle of popular Christianity around his Federalist cause. When Thomas Paine returned to America from Europe in 1802, he discovered that the popular world he had helped create had turned against him and his liberal "in fidelity." Everywhere people noted the degree to which the freethinking world of "[skeptical philosophers David] Hume & Voltaire & [the viscount of] Bolingbroke" was passing away, even among the educated gentry. As the Republic became democratized, it became evangelized.

Recognizing Christianity

Throughout the period many religious groups resisted the disintegrative effects of the Enlightenment belief in liberty of conscience and separation of church and state and urged the Republic to recognize its basis in Christianity by allowing chaplains in the Congress, proclaiming days of fasting and prayer, and by ending mail delivery on the Sabbath. In 1811, in a notable blasphemy decision of Chancellor James Kent, *The People of New York v. Ruggles*, the connection between Christianity and republicanism was acknowledge in law. Although Kent recognized that the state had no formally established church, that its constitution guaranteed freedom of religious opinion, and that it had no statute prohibiting blasphemy, he nevertheless declared that to revile with contempt the Christian religion professed by almost the whole community, as Ruggles had done, was to "strike at the roots of moral obligation and weaken the security of the social ties." That Kent was willing to rely upon religion in this way when, like many of the founding fathers, he despised religious enthusiasm and in private called Christianity a barbaric superstition is a measure of how much the traditional gentry had come to fear the social disorder of the Early Republic. Christianity, in fact, seemed to some Americans to have become the only cohesive force now holding the nation together—"the great bond of civil society," said Federalist Leverett Saltonstall of Massachusetts, "the central attraction," said [theologian] Lyman Beecher in 1815, "which must supply the deficiency of political affinity and interest."

Religion and Disunity

Yet the outpouring of religious feeling in the early decades of the nineteenth century—called the Second Great Awakening— actually did not bring people together as much as it helped to legitimate their separation and make morally possible their new participation in an impersonal marketplace. Even the New Divinity movement within New England Calvinism, despite its strong repudiation of selfishness, ultimately grounded Samuel Hopkins's famous concept of universal disinterested [that is, impartial] benevolence on the enlightened self-interest of people, and thus set credible moral limits to their acquisitive [money-making] behavior.

Others thought that religion was actually accelerating social disintegration in the new Republic by creating a "war of words and tumult of opinions" [in the words of Joseph Smith, founder of Mormonism] that rivaled the early days of the Reformation. In the decades following the Revolution the remains of traditional religious establishments were finally destroyed, and modern Christian denominationalism was born. Older churches—Congregationalists, Presbyterians, and Anglicans that had dominated eighteenth-century colonial society—were now suddenly supplanted by energetic evangelical churches—Baptists, Methodists, and entirely new groups unknown to the Old World, such as the Disciples of Christ. Everywhere the people were "awakened from the sleep of ages" and saw "for the first time that they were responsible beings" who might even be capable of bringing about their own salvation. The American Revolution accelerated the challenges to religious authority that had begun with the First Great Awakening [in the 1750s]. Just as the people were taking over their governments, so, it was said, they should take over their churches. Christianity had to be republicanized. The people were their own theologians and had no need to rely on others to tell them what to believe. We must, declared the renegade Baptist Elias Smith in 1809, be "wholly free to examine for

ourselves what is the truth, without being bound to a cat-
echism, creed, confession of faith, discipline or any rule ex-
cepting the scriptures." There had been nothing before in
America on such a scale quite like the evangelical defiance and
democratic ferment of this Second Great Awakening.

Competition Among Sects

With individuals being told that each of them was "considered
as possessing in himself or herself an original right to believe
and speak as their own conscience, between themselves and
God, may determine," religion in America became much more
personal and voluntary than it ever had been; and people
were freer to join and change religious association whenever
they wished. They thus moved from one religious group to
another in a continual search for signs, prophets, or millennial
promises that would make sense of their disrupted lives. With
no church sure of holding its communicants, competition
among the sects became fierce. Each claimed to be right, called
each other names, argued endlessly over points of doctrine,
mobbed and stoned and destroyed each other's meeting
houses. The result was a further fragmenting of Christianity.
"All Christendom has been decomposed, broken in pieces" in
this "fiery furnace of democracy," said a bewildered [U.S. sena-
tor] Harrison Gray Otis. Not only were the traditional Old
World churches fragmented but the fragments themselves
shattered in what seemed at times to be an endless process of
fission. There were not just Presbyterians, but Old and New
School Presbyterians, Cumberland Presbyterians, Springfield
Presbyterians, Reformed Presbyterians, and Associated Presbyterians; not just Baptists, but General Baptists, Regular Bap-
tists, Free Will Baptists, Separate Baptists, Dutch River Bap-
tists, Permanent Baptists, and Two-Seed-in-the-Spirit Baptists.
Some individuals cut their ties completely with the Old World
churches and gathered around a dynamic leader like Barton
Stone or Thomas Campbell. Other seekers ended up forming

churches out of single congregations, and still others simply listened in the fields to wandering preachers like the Methodist Lorenzo Dow. . . .

Moral Order

Amid this religious fragmentation, Lyman Beecher and others came to realize that making each person alone responsible for his or her salvation left nothing holding "society against depravity within and temptation without" [as Beecher put it] except the force of God's law "written upon the heart" of each individual. Only the self-restraint of individuals—their moral "character"—now remained, it seemed, to hold this burgeoning, unruly society together. To be successful in America, religion had to pre-occupy itself with morality.

Only religion, [George] Washington had said in his Farewell Address in 1796, was capable of supplying "that virtue or morality" that was "a necessary spring of popular government." From the beginning of America's republican experiment, the clergy had been repeatedly told that, whatever their doctrinal differences, "you are all united in inculcating the necessity of morals," and "from the success or failure of your exertions in the cause of virtue, we anticipate the freedom or slavery of our country." Faced with such awesome responsibility, religious groups and others responded to the cause of virtue with an evangelical zeal and clamor that went beyond what any revolutionary leader in 1776 could have imagined. The clergy could no longer rely on exposing the community's guilt through jeremiads [angry sermons]; they could no longer count on reforming merely the "better part" of the society in the expectation that it would bring the rest along; and they could no longer use government to create the right "moral effect." Ordinary people themselves had to be mobilized in the cause of virtue, through the creation of both new institutions of reform and local moral societies—"disciplined moral militia," Beecher called them.

Members of the moral societies, which are generally confined to rural villages, relied essentially on observation and
the force of local public opinion. They united among themselves, "collecting the lovers of virtue of every name," and presented "a bold front to the growing licentiousness of the day";
and then, by erecting "a citadel, from which extended observa-
tions may be made," they exerted their "influence over the
moral conduct of others," first by friendly persuasion, and
then, if that did not work, by exposing the moral delinquent
"to the penalties of the law." The hopes were high; "Character,
that dearest earthly interest of man, will thus be protected,
and the thousands who are now settling down into incurable
habits of licentiousness, will by these means be reclaimed."

Christianity Thrives in the New United States

Alexis de Tocqueville

In 1831, a French Aristocrat named Alexis de Tocqueville decided to visit the young United States, ostensibly to study prison reform but really to "see a great republic," as he wrote a friend. He examined all aspects of life in the new democracy, including religion. In the following excerpt, he describes the continued vitality of religion, and in fact asserts that this continued faith is one of the necessary preconditions for freedom and equality. At the same time, he describes the irresistible power of public opinion in shaping religion, and the increasing assertion of material well-being as a good in itself. By adapting to these new influences, Christianity actually grows stronger in the United States, he notes. Churches become less dogmatic and ritualistic, and clergymen withdraw from secular affairs. At the same time, the equality of opportunity and the breakdown of class differences actually strengthen the fundamental idea of one Creator overseeing all humanity.

De Tocqueville's Democracy in America, *published in 1835 and 1840, remains a vital source of insight on early American history. He also published a history of the French Revolution and remained an active liberal politician in France until his death in 1859.*

I have shown in a preceding chapter that men cannot do without dogmatic belief, and even that it is much to be desired that such belief should exist among them. I now add that, of all the kinds of dogmatic belief, the most desirable appears to me to be dogmatic belief in matters of religion; and this is a clear inference, even from no higher consideration than the interests of this world.

Alexis de Tocqueville, "How Religion in the United States Avails Itself of Democratic Tendencies," *Democracy in America*, vol. 1, 1835, translated by Henry Reeve, 1899.

There is hardly any human action, however particular it may be, that does not originate in some very general idea men have conceived of the Deity, of his relation to mankind, of the nature of their own souls, and of their duties to their fellow creatures. Nor can anything prevent these ideas from being the common spring from which all the rest emanates.

Men are therefore immeasurably interested in acquiring fixed ideas of God, of the soul, and of their general duties to their Creator and their fellow men; for doubt on these first principles would abandon all their actions to chance and would condemn them in some way to disorder and impotence.

This, then, is the subject on which it is most important for each of us to have fixed ideas; and unhappily it is also the subject on which it is most difficult for each of us, left to himself, to settle his opinions by the sole force of his reason. None but minds singularly free from the ordinary cares of life, minds at once penetrating, subtle, and trained by thinking, can, even with much time and care, sound the depths of these truths that are so necessary. And, indeed, we see that philosophers are themselves almost always surrounded with uncertainties; that at every step the natural light which illuminates their path grows dimmer and less secure, and that, in spite of all their efforts, they have discovered as yet only a few conflicting notions, on which the mind of man has been tossed about for thousands of years without ever firmly grasping the truth or finding novelty even in its errors. Studies of this nature are far above the average capacity of men; and, even if the majority of mankind were capable of such pursuits, it is evident that leisure to cultivate them would still be wanting. Fixed ideas about God and human nature are indispensable to the daily practice of men's lives; but the practice of their lives prevents them from acquiring such ideas.

The difficulty appears to be without a parallel. Among the sciences there are some that are useful to the mass of mankind and are within its reach; others can be approached only by the few and are not cultivated by the many, who require nothing beyond their more remote applications: but the daily practice of the science I speak of is indispensable to all, although the study of it is inaccessible to the greater number.

Necessity for Authority in Religion

General ideas respecting God and human nature are therefore the ideas above all others which it is most suitable to withdraw from the habitual action of private judgment and in which there is most to gain and least to lose by recognizing a principle of authority. The first object and one of the principal advantages of religion is to furnish to each of these fundamental questions a solution that is at once clear, precise, intelligible, and lasting, to the mass of mankind. There are religions that are false and very absurd, but it may be affirmed that any religion which remains within the circle I have just traced, without pretending to go beyond it (as many religions have attempted to do, for the purpose of restraining on every side the free movement of the human mind), imposes a salutary restraint on the intellect; and it must be admitted that, if it does not save men in another world, it is at least very conducive to their happiness and their greatness in this.

This is especially true of men living in free countries. When the religion of a people is destroyed, doubt gets hold of the higher powers of the intellect and half paralyzes all the others. Every man accustoms himself to having only confused and changing notions on the subjects most interesting to his fellow creatures and himself. His opinions are ill-defended and easily abandoned; and, in despair of ever solving by himself the hard problems respecting the destiny of man, he ignobly submits to think no more about them.

Such a condition cannot but enervate the soul, relax the springs of the will, and prepare a people for servitude. Not only does it happen in such a case that they allow their freedom to be taken from them; they frequently surrender it themselves. When there is no longer any principle of authority in religion any more than in politics, men are speedily frightened at the aspect of this unbounded independence. The constant agitation of all surrounding things alarms and exhausts them. As everything is at sea in the sphere of the mind, they determine at least that the mechanism of society shall be firm and fixed; and as they cannot resume their ancient belief, they assume a master.

For my own part, I doubt whether man can ever support at the same time complete religious independence and entire political freedom. And I am inclined to think that if faith be wanting in him, he must be subject; and if he be free, he must believe.

Equality and Isolation

Perhaps, however, this great utility of religions is still more obvious among nations where equality of conditions prevails than among others. It must be acknowledged that equality, which brings great benefits into the world, nevertheless suggests to men (as will be shown hereafter) some very dangerous propensities. It tends to isolate them from one another, to concentrate every man's attention upon himself; and it lays open the soul to an inordinate love of material gratification.

The greatest advantage of religion is to inspire diametrically contrary principles. There is no religion that does not place the object of man's desires above and beyond the treasures of earth and that does not naturally raise his soul to regions far above those of the senses. Nor is there any which does not impose on man some duties towards his kind and thus draw him at times from the contemplation of himself. This is found in the most false and dangerous religions.

Religious nations are therefore naturally strong on the very point on which democratic nations are weak; this shows of what importance it is for men to preserve their religion as their conditions become more equal.

Power of Religion in a Democratic Age

I have neither the right nor the intention of examining the supernatural means that God employs to infuse religious belief into the heart of man. I am at this moment considering religions in a purely human point of view; my object is to inquire by what means they may most easily retain their sway in the democratic ages upon which we are entering.

It has been shown that at times of general culture and equality the human mind consents only with reluctance to adopt dogmatic opinions and feels their necessity acutely only in spiritual matters. This proves, in the first place, that at such times religions ought more cautiously than at any other to confine themselves within their own precincts; for in seeking to extend their power beyond religious matters, they incur a risk of not being believed at all. The circle within which they seek to restrict the human intellect ought therefore to be carefully traced, and beyond its verge the mind should be left entirely free to its own guidance.

Mohammed professed to derive from Heaven, and has inserted in the Koran, not only religious doctrines, but political maxims, civil and criminal laws, and theories of science. The Gospel, on the contrary, speaks only of the general relations of men to God and to each other, beyond which it inculcates and imposes no point of faith. This alone, besides a thousand other reasons, would suffice to prove that the former of these religions will never long predominate in a cultivated and democratic age, while the latter is destined to retain its sway at these as at all other periods.

In continuation of this same inquiry I find that for religions to maintain their authority, humanly speaking, in democratic ages, not only must they confine themselves strictly within the circle of spiritual matters, but their power also will depend very much on the nature of the belief they inculcate, on the external forms they assume, and on the obligations they impose.

The preceding observation, that equality leads men to very general and very vast ideas, is principally to be understood in respect to religion. Men who are similar and equal in the world readily conceive the idea of the one God, governing every man by the same laws and granting to every man future happiness on the same conditions. The idea of the unity of mankind constantly leads them back to the idea of the unity of the Creator; while on the contrary in a state of society where men are broken up into very unequal ranks, they are apt to devise as many deities as there are nations, castes, classes, or families, and to trace a thousand private roads to heaven.

It cannot be denied that Christianity itself has felt, to some extent, the influence that social and political conditions exercise on religious opinions. . . .

Informality Preferred

In speaking of philosophical method among the Americans I have shown that nothing is more repugnant to the human mind in an age of equality than the idea of subjection to forms. Men living at such times are impatient of figures; to their eyes, symbols appear to be puerile [childish] artifices used to conceal or to set off truths that should more naturally be bared to the light of day; they are unmoved by ceremonial observances and are disposed to attach only a secondary importance to the details of public worship.

Those who have to regulate the external forms of religion in a democratic age should pay a close attention to these natural propensities of the human mind in order not to run counter to them unnecessarily.

I firmly believe in the necessity of forms, which fix the human mind in the contemplation of abstract truths and aid it in embracing them warmly and holding them with firmness. Nor do I suppose that it is possible to maintain a religion without external observances; but, on the other hand, I am persuaded that in the ages upon which we are entering it would be peculiarly dangerous to multiply them beyond measure, and that they ought rather to be limited to as much as is absolutely necessary to perpetuate the doctrine itself, which is the substance of religion, of which the ritual is only the form. A religion which became more insistent in details, more inflexible, and more burdened with small observances during the time that men became more equal would soon find itself limited to a band of fanatic zealots in the midst of a skeptical multitude.

I anticipate the objection that, as all religions have general and eternal truths for their object, they cannot thus shape themselves to the shifting inclinations of every age without forfeiting their claim to certainty in the eyes of mankind. To this I reply again that the principal opinions which constitute a creed, and which theologians call articles of faith, must be very carefully distinguished from the accessories connected with them. Religions are obliged to hold fast to the former, whatever be the peculiar spirit of the age; but they should take good care not to bind themselves in the same manner to the latter at a time when everything is in transition and when the mind, accustomed to the moving pageant of human affairs, reluctantly allows itself to be fixed on any point. The permanence of external and secondary things seems to me to have a chance of enduring only when civil society is itself static; under any other circumstances I am inclined to regard it as dangerous.

The Love of Well-Being

We shall see that of all the passions which originate in or are fostered by equality, there is one which it renders peculiarly intense, and which it also infuses into the heart of every man;

75

I mean the love of well-being. The taste for well-being is the prominent and indelible feature of democratic times.

It may be believed that a religion which should undertake to destroy so deep-seated a passion would in the end be destroyed by it; and if it attempted to wean men entirely from the contemplation of the good things of this world in order to devote their faculties exclusively to the thought of another, it may be foreseen that the minds of men would at length escape its grasp, to plunge into the exclusive enjoyment of present and material pleasures.

The chief concern of religion is to purify, to regulate, and to restrain the excessive and exclusive taste for well-being that men feel in periods of equality; but it would be an error to attempt to overcome it completely or to eradicate it. Men cannot be cured of the love of riches, but they may be persuaded to enrich themselves by none but honest means.

This brings me to a final consideration, which comprises, as it were, all the others. The more the conditions of men are equalized and assimilated to each other, the more important is it for religion, while it carefully abstains from the daily turmoil of secular affairs, not needlessly to run counter to the ideas that generally prevail or to the permanent interests that exist in the mass of the people. For as public opinion grows to be more and more the first and most irresistible of existing powers, the religious principle has no external support strong enough to enable it long to resist its attacks. This is not less true of a democratic people ruled by a despot than of a republic. In ages of equality kings may often command obedience, but the majority always commands belief; to the majority, therefore, deference is to be paid in whatever is not contrary to the faith.

Role of Clergy

I showed in the first Part of this work how the American clergy stand aloof from secular affairs. This is the most obvious but not the only example of their self-restraint. In America religion is a distinct sphere, in which the priest is sovereign, but out of which he takes care never to go. Within its limits he is master of the mind; beyond them he leaves men to themselves and surrenders them to the independence and instability that belong to their nature and their age. I have seen no country in which Christianity is clothed with fewer forms, figures, and observances than in the United States, or where it presents more distinct, simple, and general notions to the mind. Although the Christians of America are divided into a multitude of sects, they all look upon their religion in the same light. This applies to Roman Catholicism as well as to the other forms of belief. There are no Roman Catholic priests who show less taste for the minute individual observances, for extraordinary or peculiar means of salvation, or who cling more to the spirit and less to the letter of the law than the Roman Catholic priests of the United States. Nowhere is that doctrine of the church which prohibits the worship reserved to God alone from being offered to the saints more clearly inculcated or more generally followed. Yet the Roman Catholics of America are very submissive and very sincere.

Another remark is applicable to the clergy of every communion. The American ministers of the Gospel do not attempt to draw or to fix all the thoughts of man upon the life to come; they are willing to surrender a portion of his heart to the cares of the present, seeming to consider the goods of this world as important, though secondary, objects. If they take no part themselves in productive labor, they are at least interested in its progress and they applaud its results, and while they never cease to point to the other world as the great object of the hopes and fears of the believer, they do not forbid him honestly to court prosperity in this. Far from attempting to show that these things are distinct and contrary to one another, they study rather to find out on what point they are most nearly and closely connected.

All the American clergy know and respect the intellectual supremacy exercised by the majority; they never sustain any but necessary conflicts with it. They take no share in the altercations of parties, but they readily adopt the general opinions of their country and their age, and they allow themselves to be borne away without opposition in the current of feeling and opinion by which everything around them is carried along. They endeavor to amend their contemporaries, but they do not quit fellowship with them. Public opinion is therefore never hostile to them; it rather supports and protects them, and their belief owes its authority at the same time to the strength which is its own and to that which it borrows from the opinions of the majority.

Thus it is that by respecting all democratic tendencies not absolutely contrary to herself and by making use of several of them for her own purposes, religion sustains a successful struggle with that spirit of individual independence which is her most dangerous opponent.

CHAPTER 3

The Intersection of Government and Religion

Chapter Preface

The American Revolution unleashed many forces, and it was difficult for contemporaries to keep up. A rural, monarchical, traditional society gave way to the forces of industrialization, democracy, and urbanization, and a dramatic rise in immigration. Some of the Founders, such as Thomas Jefferson and John Adams, expected that religion would also change and that the more intellectually oriented Unitarianism would replace the more traditional, "superstitious" versions of Christianity.

The Church of England, which had dominated the southern states, was discredited by the Revolution, and it easily lost its dominant position in those states. Others states were slower, however; Massachusetts did not disestablish its Congregationalist Church until 1833. Still, the trend was obvious, and events at the federal level were even more encouraging. The people who ratified the Constitution insisted on an amendment that banned any national establishment of religion, and the Constitution itself banned any religious test for those seeking federal office. Jefferson himself, despite constant accusations that he was an atheist and unfit to be a leader, won the presidency in 1800 and lived to see the demise of the Federalist Party that had opposed him largely on those grounds.

At the same time, a great many Americans were undergoing a religious upsurge known as the Second Great Awakening. Revivals led by inspirational preachers caused a renewed interest in both religion and social activism throughout New England. In New York, charismatic prophets went further, founding entirely new religions, most notably the Church of Jesus Christ of Latter-Day Saints, more commonly referred to as Mormonism. To the South, especially in the Appalachian region, "camp meetings" lasting several days brought skilled preachers to isolated communities, creating a wave of new converts that swelled the ranks of Methodist, Presbyterian, and other evangelical churches.

These conversions would dramatically affect the political life of the nineteenth century as well. Highly charged issues like the abolition of slavery and the Temperance Movement that sought to ban alcohol had a strong religious component, and these conversions swelled the ranks of these movements. Many new converts and newly inspired churchgoers went into the slums and poor rural areas, and many were stunned and outraged by the sharp divisions between rich and poor, leading to calls for social justice. Many of these movements were led by women, providing a training ground for the women who would demand the right to vote, first in the states and then in federal elections.

Combined with all this was a dramatic influx of immigrants, including unprecedented numbers of Catholics and Jews. This created a dilemma for the generation of the Founders. Bigotry against both groups was widespread, but so was the desire to overcome the ancient hatreds that split Europeans. In terms of numbers, Catholics posed the bigger challenge, and by creating a system of parochial schools, they would eventually pose a legal challenge in terms of whether government could provide any support to those schools.

Some actively opposed these new immigrants, retreating into anti-Semitic and anti-Catholic organizations and political parties. Others, however, embraced the separation of church and state even more strongly, precisely because of fear that Catholic voters and leaders, believed to be beholden to their pope before all else, would try to impose their religion on America.

Voters Should Insist on Christian Leaders

Ezra Stiles Ely

*The First Amendment to the U.S. Constitution guarantees free-
dom of religion and bans any religious test for those seeking federal office. That clause does not bind American voters, however,
who can apply any test they want to a candidate. In 1827, a
prominent Presbyterian minister and political activist named
Ezra Stiles Ely called on American Christians to exercise that
power. In a sermon delivered on the Fourth of July, he called
upon Christians to vote only for Christians, to demand a government that was especially friendly to Christianity, and to hold
politicians to a moral code based on Christian principles. Further, to ensure this, he proposed the creation of a Christian party
that would hold people seeking elected office to these principles.
The sermon was reprinted and widely circulated; so widely that
Ely's friend, then-presidential candidate Andrew Jackson, felt
moved to write a letter warning Ely about the dangers to liberty
in this approach. Ely did not agree, and he remained a leading
voice for Christian government until his death in 1861. He is
particularly well known for advocating Sabbatarianism: the outlawing of business, public transportation, and indeed all public
services on the Sabbath.*

We have assembled, fellow citizens, on the anniversary of
our Nation's birth day, in a rational and religious manner, to celebrate our independence of all foreign domination,
and the goodness of God in making us a free and happy
people. On what subject can I, on the present occasion, insist
with more propriety, than on the duty of all the rulers and
citizens of these United States in the exercise and enjoyment
of all their political rights, to honour the Lord Jesus Christ.

Ezra Stiles Ely, "A Discourse, &c," *The Duty of Christian Freemen to Elect Christian
Rulers*, Philadelphia: William F. Geddes, 1828.

Let it then be distinctly stated and fearlessly maintained IN THE FIRST PLACE, that every member of this Christian nation, from the highest to the lowest, ought to serve the Lord with fear, and yield his sincere homage to the Son of God. Every ruler *should* be an avowed and a sincere friend of Christianity. He should know and believe the doctrines of our holy religion, and act in conformity with its precepts. This *he ought* to do; because as a man he is required to serve the Lord; and as a public ruler he is called upon by divine authority to "kiss the Son." The commandment contained in Proverbs iii. 6. "*in all thy ways acknowledge him,*" includes public as well as private ways, and political no less than domestic ways. It is addressed equally to the man who rules, and to the person who is subject to authority. If we may not disown our God and Saviour in *any* situation, it will follow that we are to own him in *every* situation. Infinite wisdom has taught us, that *he who ruleth over men must be just, ruling in the fear of God.* No *Christian* can gainsay this decision. Let all then admit, that our civil rulers ought to act a religious part in all the relations which they sustain. Indeed, they ought pre-eminently to commit their way unto the Lord that he may direct their steps; delight themselves in him, and wait patiently for him; because by their example, if good, they can do more good than private, less known citizens; and if evil, more harm. Their official station is a talent entrusted to them for usefulness, for which they must give account to their Maker. They are like a city set on a hill, which cannot be hid; and it is a fact indisputable, that wickedness in high places does more harm than in obscurity.

Rulers Should Be Christian

I would guard, however, against misunderstanding and misrepresentation, when I state, that all our rulers ought in their official stations to serve the Lord Jesus Christ. I do not wish any religious test to be prescribed by constitution, and proposed to a man on his acceptance of any public trust. Neither can any intelligent friend of his country and of true religion desire the establishment of any one religious sect by civil law. Let the religion of the Bible rest on that everlasting rock, and on those spiritual laws, on which Jehovah has founded his kingdom: let Christianity by the spirit of Christ in her members support herself: let Church and State be for ever distinct: but, still, let the doctrines and precepts of Christ govern all men, in all their relations and employments. If a ruler is not a Christian he ought to be one, in this land of evangelical light, without delay; and he ought, being a follower of Jesus, to honour him even as he honours the FATHER. In this land of religious freedom, what should hinder a civil magistrate from believing the gospel, and professing faith in Christ, any more than any other man? If the Chief Magistrate of a nation may be an irreligious man, with impunity, who may not? It seems to be generally granted, that our political leaders in the national and state governments ought not to be notoriously profane, drunken, abandoned men in their moral conduct; but if they may not be injurious to themselves and their fellow men, who shall give them permission to contemn [disrespect] God? If they ought to be just towards men, ought they not also to abstain from robbing God, and to render unto him that honour which is HIS due?

Our rulers, like any other members of the community, who are under law to God as rational beings, and under law to Christ, since they have the light of divine revelation, ought to search the scriptures, assent to the truth, profess faith in Christ, keep the Sabbath holy to God, pray in private and in the domestic circle, attend on the public ministry of the word, be baptized, and celebrate the Lord's supper. None of our rulers have the consent of their Maker, that they should be Pagans, Socinians [a contemporary heretical Christian sect], Mussulmen [Muslims], Deists, the opponents of Christianity; and a religious people should never think of giving them permission, as public officers, to be and do, what they might not lawfully be and do, as private individuals. . . .

God, my hearers, requires a Christian faith, a Christian profession, and a Christian practice of all our public men; and we as Christian citizens ought, by the publication of our opinions, to require the same.

Christians Should Vote for Christians

SECONDLY, Since it is the duty of all our rulers to serve the Lord and kiss the Son of God, it must be most manifestly the duty of all our Christian fellow-citizens to honour the Lord Jesus Christ and promote Christianity by electing and supporting as public officers the friends of our blessed Saviour. Let it only be granted, that Christians have the same rights and privileges in exercising the elective franchise, which are here accorded to Jews and Infidels, and we ask no other evidence to show, that those who prefer a Christian ruler, may unite in supporting him, in preference to any one of a different character. It shall cheerfully be granted, that every citizen is eligible to every office, whatever may be his religious opinions and moral character; and that every one may constitutionally support any person whom he may *choose*; but it will not hence follow, that he is without accountability to his Divine Master for his choice; or that he may lay aside all his Christian principles and feelings when he selects his ticket and presents it at the polls. "*In all* thy ways acknowledge him," is a maxim which should dwell in a Christian's mind on the day of a public election as much as on the Sabbath; and which should govern him when conspiring with others to honour Christ, either at the Lord's table, or in the election of a Chief Magistrate. In elucidating the duty of private Christians in relation to the choice of their civil rulers, it seems to me necessary to remark,

1. That every Christian who has the right and the opportunity of exercising the elective franchise ought to do it. Many

pious people feel so much disgust at the manner in which elections are conducted, from the first nomination to the closing of the polls, that they relinquish their right of voting for years together. But if all *pious* people were to conduct thus, then our rulers would be wholly elected by the *impious*. If all *good men* are to absent themselves from elections, then the *bad* will have the entire transaction of our public business.

If the wise, the prudent, the tempests, the friends of God and of their country do not endeavour to control our elections, they will be controlled by others; and if *one* good man may, without any reasonable excuse, absent himself, then *all* may. Fellow Christians, the love of Christ and of our fellow-men should forbid us to yield the choice of our civil rulers into the hands of selfish hunters, and the miserable tools of their party politics. . . .

A Christian Party

I propose, fellow-citizens, a new sort of union, or, if you please, *a Christian party in politics*, which I am exceedingly desirous all good men in our country should join: not by *subscribing a constitution* and the formation of a new society, to be added to the scores which now exist; but by adopting, avowing, and determining to act upon, truly religious principles in all civil matters. I am aware that the true Christians of our country are divided into many different denominations; who have, alas! too many points of jealousy and collision; still, a union to a very great extent, and for the most valuable purposes is not impracticable. For,

2. All Christians, of all denominations, may, and ought to, agree in determining, that they will never wittingly support for any public office, any person whom they know or believe to sustain, at the time of his proposed election, a bad moral character. In this, thousands of moralists, who profess no experimental acquaintance with Christianity, might unite and co-operate with *our Christian party*. And surely, it is not im-

possible, nor unreasonable for all classes of Christians to say within themselves, no man that we have reason to think is a liar, thief, gambler, murderer, debauchee, spendthrift, or openly immoral person in any way, shall have our support at any election. REFORMATION should not only be allowed, but encouraged; for it would be requiring too much to insist upon it, that a candidate for office *shall always have sustained an unblemished moral character*, and it would be unchristian not to forgive and support one who has proved his repentance by recantation and a considerable course of new obedience. . . .

A Right to Pro-Christian Government

3. All who profess to be Christians of any denomination ought to agree that they will support no man as a candidate for any office, who is not professedly friendly to Christianity, and a believer in divine Revelation. We do not say that true or even pretended Christianity shall be made a constitutional test of admission to office; but we do affirm that Christians may in their elections lawfully prefer the avowed friends of the Christian religion to Turks [Muslims], Jews and Infidels. Turks, indeed, might naturally prefer Turks, if they could elect them; and Infidels might prefer Infidels; and I should not wonder if a conscientious Jew should prefer a ruler of his own religious faith; but it would be passing strange if a Christian should not desire the election of one friendly to his own system of religion. While every religious system is tolerated in our country, and no one is established by law, it is still possible for me to think, that the friend of Christianity will make a much better governor of this commonwealth or President of the United States, than the advocate of Theism or Polytheism. We will not pretend to search the heart; but surely all sects of Christians may agree in opinion, that it is more desirable to have a Christian than a Jew, Mohammedan, or Pagan, in any civil office; and they may accordingly settle it in their minds, that they will never vote for any one to fill any office in the nation

or state, who does not profess to receive the Bible as the rule of his faith. If three or four of the most numerous denominations of Christians in the United States, the Presbyterians, the Baptists, the Methodists and Congregationalists for instance, should act upon this principle, our country would never be dishonoured with an *avowed infidel* in her national cabinet or capitol. The Presbyterians alone could bring *half a million of electors* into the field, in opposition to any known advocate of Deism, Socinianism, or any species of avowed hostility to the truth of Christianity. If to the denominations above named we add the members of the Protestant Episcopal church in our country, the electors of these five classes of true Christians, united in the sole requisition of apparent friendship to Christianity in every candidate for office whom they will support, could govern every public election in our country, without infringing in the least upon the charter of our civil liberties. To these might be added, in this State and in Ohio, the numerous German Christians, and in New York and New Jersey the members of the Reformed Dutch Church, who are all zealous for the fundamental truths of Christianity. What should prevent us from co-operating in such a union as this? Let a man be of good moral character and let him profess to believe in and advocate the Christian religion, and we can all support him. At one time he will be a Baptist, at another an Episcopalian, at another a Methodist, at another a Presbyterian of the American, Scotch, Irish, Dutch, or German stamp, and always a friend to our common Christianity. Why then should we ever suffer an enemy, an open and known enemy of the true religion of Christ, to enact our laws or fill the executive chair? Our Christian rulers will not oppress Jews or Infidels; they will *kiss the Son and serve the Lord*; while we have the best security for their fidelity to our republican, and I may say scriptural, forms of government.

It deprives no man of his right for me to prefer a Christian to an Infidel. If Infidels were the most numerous electors, they would doubtless elect men of their own sentiments; and unhappily such men not unfrequently get into power in this country, in which ninety-nine hundredths of the people are believers in the divine origin and authority of the Christian religion. If hundreds of thousands of our fellow citizens should agree with us in an effort to elect men to public office who read the Bible, profess to believe it, reverence the Sabbath, attend public worship, and sustain a good moral character, who could complain? Have we not as much liberty to be the supporters of the Christian cause by our votes, as others have to support anti-christian men and measures?

Let us awake, then, fellow Christians, to our sacred duty to our Divine Master; and let us have no rulers, with our consent and co-operation, who are not known to be avowedly Christians.

Anti-Catholicism Impels
the Separation of Church
and State

Philip Hamburger

The separation of church and state in the United States is usually seen in terms of secular worries about religious dominance in general. In an unusual thesis, Philip Hamburger finds a more specific reason. As he explains, Protestant worries about Catholicism changed a doctrine of religious liberty into a separation of church and state. In building a new democratic society, a number of Protestants began to question the traditional authority of churches and clergy. Quite a few saw Catholic immigrants as dangerously submissive to their bishops and to a foreign leader, the pope. A large number of influential Protestants began to identify "true Americanism" with independence from control by churches of any kind. The individualism and specialization in other aspects of their lives only reinforced this tendency, making religion a separate, private matter that was not supposed to intrude on public, political issues.

Philip Hamburger is the Friedman Professor of Law at the Columbia University Law School. He specializes in constitutional law and history. Prior to this appointment, he was director of the Legal History Program at the University of Chicago School of Law.

In order to trace how American religious liberty came to be conceived as a separation between church and state, [one] must examine how the idea of separation flourished among broader cultural and social developments, including ideals of

Philip Hamburger, "Introduction," *Separation of Church and State*, Cambridge, MA: Harvard University Press, 2002, pp. 14–17. Copyright © 2002 by the President and Fellows of Harvard College. All rights reserved. Reprinted by permission of Harvard University Press.

individual independence, fears of Catholicism, and various types of specialization. Although often omitted from the history of religious liberty, these more general tendencies can suggest much about the growing popularity of separation.

Separation often attracted Protestants who felt individualistic fears of religious groups. Many nineteenth- and twentieth-century Americans worried about the power of government. In addition, however, numerous Protestants felt anxiety about nongovernmental groups and hierarchies, particularly churches and their clergies. From the perspective of these Protestants, the claims of authority made by churches—even if merely claims of moral rather than legal authority—could be oppressive and dangerous to the freedom of individuals. Accordingly, in the nineteenth and twentieth centuries separation often appealed to Americans who thought of themselves as mentally independent—particularly to those who conceived of themselves as independent of their churches. Of course, in America's ever more secular society, separation also attracted expanding numbers of nonreligious persons. More generally and pervasively, however, it appealed to those whose liberal theology or whose sense of distance from communal, clerical religion led them to think of themselves as intellectually independent of any ecclesiastical dictates.

America's Protestant Character

This distrust of church authority increasingly permeated American Protestantism and its often nativist [anti-immigrant] critique of the Catholic Church. Fearful of Catholic immigrants, many native-born Protestants emphasized the Protestant character of their American identity. In particular, they adopted heightened expectations of intellectual independence. Believing that this individual independence was essential for both genuine religion and American citizenship, they demanded that Catholics adhere to hyper-individualistic ideals of mental freedom. In this spirit, nativist Protestants worried that the pope's claims of ecclesiastical authority would stultify the minds of Catholics, rendering them unfit to vote and giving the Church an influence that would allow it to threaten freedom through the institutions of republican government. Against these and related dangers, *growing numbers* of Protestant Americans demanded a *separation of church and state.* Thus nativist demands for mental independence and for a separation between church and state took aim at Catholics for their failure to adopt supposedly Protestant and American beliefs. In such ways, religious liberty itself—even an unusually individualistic conception of it—was often employed to demand conformity.

Role of Specialization

The separation of church and state had particular appeal in an age of specialization. Separation often attracted individuals who—whether in fact or in their minds—divided their lives into distinct activities and sought to maintain their freedom within each such activity by restricting the demands of the others. [Thomas] Jefferson, his allies, and many subsequent Americans attempted, on occasion, to limit religion to a private, personal, or nonpolitical realm so that it would not intrude too much (whether by force of law or only by force of argument) on various other aspects of their lives. To such Americans, the moral claims of an entirely voluntary, disestablished church could seem *threatening.* Accordingly, increasing numbers of Americans attempted to escape these constraining demands of churches by welcoming various separations between organized religion and other facets of their lives, particularly a separation between church and state.

Ironically, however, religion was not so easily confined. The very parties and groups that in the nineteenth century most vigorously condemned church participation in politics simultaneously encouraged a much more direct and individualized pursuit of religious yearnings in this secular arena and, in this way, rechanneled profoundly religious passions and aspirations from Christian churches to egalitarian politics. Their efforts, however, probably were only part of a broader displacement of aspirations—a transference of religiosity to various specialized, secular activities—that may have been almost inevitable with the fragmentation of society and the decline of localized "social worship." In their increasingly fractured and secular circumstances, Americans who found their desires for purity and transcendence unsatisfied in the communal worship of traditional religion often pursued these goals in more specialized endeavors but most commonly in politics. Thus the separation of church and state may have been part of a specialization of religion, politics, and much of the rest of life that simultaneously contributed to the secularization of most activities and left many Americans to pursue in their specialized, secular endeavors the sort of yearnings they once more typically satisfied in their religious groups.

These cultural and social contexts—ranging from fears of group authority to the displacement of yearnings—suggest that the evolution of American religious liberty into a separation of church and state cannot be understood simply as the product of great men, whether Roger Williams, Thomas Jefferson, or [late-twentieth-century Supreme Court justice] Hugo Black. Nor can it be understood merely as an institutional development, whether in the documents of the U.S. Constitution or in the opinions of the U.S. Supreme Court. Instead, the redefinition of American religious liberty as a separation of church and state needs to be considered within the context of America's broader ideas, culture, and society. Amid these wider circumstances, including changing popular perceptions and fears, Americans gradually transformed their understanding of religious liberty. Increasingly, Americans conceived their freedom to require an independence from churches, and they feared the demands of one church in particular [that is, the Roman Catholic Church]. To limit such threats, Americans called for a separation of church and state, and eventually the U.S. Supreme Court gave their new conception of religious liberty the force of law.

Mormonism Must Change or Be Outlawed

U.S. Congress

In a highly unusual move, the U.S. Congress actually disincorporated (that is, dissolved as a legal entity) a church, the Church of Jesus Christ of Latter-Day Saints, often known as the Mormon Church, in 1887. It seized church property and in effect forced Mormons to renounce one of their religion's doctrines: polygamy. Polygamy, the practice of a man taking more than one wife, was deemed an unlawful and unacceptable act by the federal government. Mormons dominated the Utah Territory and in practice declined to prosecute "plural marriages." Congress's Edmunds-Tucker Act was an attempt to overrule that practice. It emphatically outlawed polygamy and gave federal authorities wide-ranging powers to enforce the law, specifically removing a loophole that allowed prosecution for adultery only on the complaint of a husband or wife. It also overturned territorial legislation that incorporated the Church, seized all church properties valued at more than fifty thousand dollars, required "plural wives" to testify against their husbands, and even required potential voters to swear to uphold the laws of the United States and to renounce polygamy. In 1890, the issue was resolved when the Mormon Church officially renounced polygamy, but the Edmunds-Tucker Act was not officially repealed until 1978.

Senator George F. Edmunds of Vermont (1828–1919) was the driving force behind this act. He is otherwise known for authoring the Sherman Antitrust Act, which limited industrial monopolies. Representative John Randolph Tucker of Virginia (1823–1897) was the bill's cosponsor.

U.S. Congress, "Edmunds-Tucker Act, US Code Title 48 & 1461," 1887.

B e it enacted by the Senate and House of Representatives of the United States of America in Congress assembled, SEC. 1. That in any proceeding or examination before a grand jury, a judge, justice, or a United States commissioner, or a court, in any prosecution for bigamy, polygamy, or unlawful cohabitation, under any statute of the United States, the lawful husband or wife of the person accused shall be a competent witness, and may be called, but shall not be compelled to testify in such proceeding, examination, or prosecution without the consent of the husband or wife, as the case may be; and such witness shall not be permitted to testify as to any statement or communication made by either husband or wife to each other, during the existence of the marriage relation, deemed confidential at common law.

SEC. 2. That in any prosecution for bigamy, polygamy, or unlawful cohabitation, under any statute of the United States, whether before a United States commissioner, justice, judge, a grand jury, or any court, an attachment for any witness may be issued by the court, judge, or commissioner, without a previous subpoena, compelling the immediate attendance of such witness, when it shall appear by oath or affirmation, to the commissioner, justice, judge, or court, as the case may be, that there is reasonable ground to believe that such witness will unlawfully fail to obey a subpoena issued and served in the usual course in such cases; and in such case the usual witness-fee shall be paid to such witness so attached: *Provided*, That the person so attached may at any time secure his or her discharge from custody by executing a recognizance with sufficient surety, conditioned for the appearance of such person at the proper time, as a witness in the cause or proceeding wherein the attachment may be issued.

SEC. 3. That whoever commits adultery shall be punished by imprisonment in the penitentiary not exceeding three years; and when the act is committed between a married woman and a man who is unmarried, both parties to such act shall be deemed guilty of adultery; and when such act is committed between a married man and a woman who is unmarried, the man shall be deemed guilty of adultery.

SEC. 4. That if any person related to another person within and not including the fourth degree of consanguinity [kinship] computed according to the rules of the civil law, shall marry or cohabit with, or have sexual intercourse with such other so related person, knowing her or him to be within said degree of relationship, the person so offending shall be deemed guilty of incest, and, on conviction thereof, shall be punished by imprisonment in the penitentiary not less than three years and not more than fifteen years.

SEC. 5. That if an unmarried man or woman commit fornication, each of them shall be punished by imprisonment not exceeding six months, or by fine not exceeding one hundred dollars.

Laws Overturned

SEC. 6. That all laws of the legislative assembly of the Territory of Utah which provide that prosecutions for adultery can only be commenced on the complaint of the husband or wife are hereby disapproved and annulled; and all prosecutions for adultery may hereafter be instituted in the same way that prosecutions for other crimes are.

SEC. 7. That commissioners appointed by the supreme court and district courts in the Territory of Utah shall possess and may exercise all the powers and jurisdiction that are or may be possessed or exercised by justices of the peace in said Territory under the laws thereof, and the same powers conferred by law on commissioners appointed by circuit courts of the United States.

SEC. 8. That the marshal of said Territory of Utah, and his deputies, shall possess and may exercise all the powers in executing the laws of the United States or of said Territory, possessed and exercised by sheriffs, constables, and their deputies as peace officers; and each of them shall cause all offenders against the law, in his view, to enter into recognizance to keep the peace and to appear at the next term of the court having jurisdiction of the case, and to commit to jail in case of failure to give such recognizance. They shall quell and suppress assaults and batteries, riots, routs, affrays, and insurrections.

SEC. 9. That every ceremony of marriage, or in the nature of a marriage ceremony, of any kind, in any of the Territories of the United States, whether either or both or more of the parties to such ceremony be lawfully competent to be the subjects of such marriage or ceremony or not, shall be certified by a certificate stating the fact and nature of such ceremony, the full names of each of the parties concerned, and the full name of every officer, priest, and person, by whatever style or designation called or known, in any way taking part in the performance of such ceremony, which certificate shall be drawn up and signed by the parties to such ceremony and by every officer, priest, and person taking part in the performance of such ceremony, and shall be by the officer, priest, or other person solemnizing such marriage or ceremony filed in the office of the probate court, or, if there be none, in the office of court having probate powers in the county or district in which such ceremony shall take place, for record, and shall be immediately recorded, and be at all times subject to inspection as other public records. Such certificate, or the record thereof, or a duly certified copy of such record, shall be prima facie evidence of the facts required by this act to be stated therein, in any proceeding, civil or criminal, in which the matter shall be drawn in question. Any person who shall willfully violate any of the provisions of this section shall be deemed guilty of a misdemeanor, and shall, on conviction thereof, be punished by a fine of not more than one thousand dollars, or by imprisonment not longer than two years, or by both said punishments, in the discretion of the court.

SEC 10. That nothing in this act shall be held to prevent the proof of marriages, whether lawful or unlawful, by any evidence now legally admissible for that purpose. . . .

Dissolution of the Church

SEC. 17. That the acts of the legislative assembly of the Territory of Utah incorporating, continuing, or providing for the corporation known as the Church of Jesus Christ of Latter-Day Saints, and the ordinance of the so-called general assembly of . . . incorporating the Church of Jesus Christ of Latter-Day Saints, so far as the same may now have legal force and validity, are hereby disapproved and annulled, and the said corporation, in so far as it may now have, or pretend to have, any legal existence, is hereby dissolved. That it shall be the duty of the Attorney-General of the United States to cause such proceedings to be taken in the supreme court of the Territory of Utah as shall be proper to execute the foregoing provisions of this section and to wind up the affairs of said corporation conformably to law; and in such proceedings the court shall have power, and it shall be its duty, to make such decree or decrees as shall be proper to effectuate the transfer of the title to real property now held and used by said corporation for places of worship, and parsonages connected therewith, and burial grounds, and of the description mentioned in the proviso to section thirteen of this act and in section twenty-six of this act, to the respective trustees mentioned in section twenty-six of this act; and for the purposes of this section said court shall have all the powers of a court of equity. . . .

A Special Oath

SEC. 24. That every male person twenty-one years of age resident in the Territory of Utah shall, as a condition precedent to his right to register or vote at any election in said Territory, take, and subscribe an oath or affirmation, before the registration officer of his voting precinct, that he is over twenty-one years of age, and has resided in the Territory of Utah for six months then last passed and in the precinct for one month immediately preceding the date thereof, and that he is a native-born (or naturalized, as the case may be) citizen of the United States, and further state in such oath or affirmation his full name, with his age, place of business, his status, whether single or married, and, if married, the name of his lawful wife, and that he will support the Constitution of the United States and will faithfully obey the laws thereof and especially will obey the [Edmunds-Tucker] act of Congress approved March twenty-second eighteen hundred and eighty-two, entitled "An act to amend section fifty-three hundred and fifty-two of the Revised Statutes of the United States, in reference to bigamy, and for other purposes," and will also obey this act in respect of the crimes in said act defined and forbidden, and that he will not, directly or indirectly, aid or abet, counsel or advise, any other person to commit any of said crimes. Such registration officer is authorized to administer said oath or affirmation; and all such oaths or affirmations shall be by him delivered to the clerk of the probate court of the proper county, and shall be deemed public records therein. But if any election shall occur in said Territory before the next revision of the registration lists as required by law, the said oath or affirmation shall be administered by the presiding judge of the election precinct on or before the day of election. As a condition precedent to the right to hold office in or under said Territory, the officer, before entering on the duties of his office, shall take and subscribe an oath or affirmation declaring his full name, with his age, place of business, his status, whether married or single, and, if married, the name of his lawful wife, and that he will support the Constitution of the United States and will faithfully obey the laws thereof, and especially will obey the act of Congress approved March twenty-second, eighteen hundred and eighty-two, entitled "An act to amend section fifty-three hundred and fifty-two of the Revised Statutes of the United States, in reference to bigamy, and for other purposes," and will also obey this act in respect of the crimes in said act defined and forbidden, and that he will not, directly or in directly, aid or abet, counsel or advise, any other person to commit any of said crimes; which oath or affirmation shall be recorded in the proper office and indorsed on the commission or certificate of appointment. All grand and petit jurors in said Territory shall take the same oath or affirmation, to be administered, in writing or orally, in the proper court. No person shall be entitled to vote in any election in said Territory, or be capable of jury service, or hold any office of trust or emolument in said Territory who shall not have taken the oath or affirmation aforesaid. No person who shall have been convicted of any crime under this act, or under the act of Congress aforesaid approved March twenty second, eighteen hundred and eighty-two, or who shall be a polygamist, or who shall associate or cohabit polygamously with persons of the other sex, shall be entitled to vote in any election in said Territory, or be capable of jury service, or to hold any office of trust or emolument in said Territory.

SEC. 25. That the office of Territorial superintendent of district schools created by the laws of Utah is hereby abolished; and it shall be the duty of the supreme court of said Territory to appoint a commissioner of schools, who shall possess and exercise all the powers and duties heretofore imposed by the laws of said Territory upon the Territorial superintendent of district schools, and who shall receive the same salary and compensation, which shall be paid out of the treasury of said Territory; and the laws of the Territory of Utah providing for the method of election and appointment of such Territorial superintendent of district schools are hereby suspended until the further action of Congress shall be had in respect thereto. The said superintendent shall have power to prohibit the use in any district school of any book of a sectarian character or otherwise unsuitable. Said superintendent shall collect and classify statistics and other information respecting the district and other schools in said Territory, showing their progress, the whole number of children of school age, the number who attend school in each year in the respective counties, the average length of time of their attendance, the number of teachers and the compensation paid to the same, the number of teachers who are Mormons, the number who are so-called gentiles, the number of children of Mormon parents and the number of children of so-called gentile parents, and their respective average attendance at school; all of which statistics and information shall be annually reported to Congress, through the governor of said Territory and the Department of the Interior.

SEC. 26. That all religious societies, sects, and congregations shall have the right to have and to hold, through trustees appointed by any court exercising probate powers in a Territory, only on the nomination of the authorities of such society, sect, or congregation, so much real property for the erection or use of houses of worship, and for such parsonages and burial grounds as shall be necessary for the convenience and use of the several congregations of such religious society, sect, or congregation.

The History of "In God We Trust"

U.S. Department of the Treasury

The separation of church and state is a complex idea in a society as religious as the United States. For some, it demands governmental neutrality toward a belief in God or any other deity. This has never been accepted by many others, and one glaring exception to the rule can be found in every home and business in America. That is the phrase "In God We Trust," the official motto of the United States, which can be seen on every coin minted in the United States. On its official Web site, the U.S. Department of the Treasury provides an account of the history of this motto. Urged on by many devout persons—in particular, the Reverend M.R. Watkinson of Pennsylvania—in 1861 secretary of the treasury Salmon P. Chase ordered that the director of the U.S. Mint create a motto recognizing the role of God that would be used on American coins. Eventually the mint settled on "In God We Trust." This required congressional approval, which came in 1864, and in 1956 this phrase became the national motto of the United States.

The motto IN GOD WE TRUST was placed on United States coins largely because of the increased religious sentiment existing during the Civil War. Secretary of the Treasury Salmon P. Chase received many appeals from devout persons throughout the country, urging that the United States recognize the Deity on United States coins. From Treasury Department records, it appears that the first such appeal came in a letter dated November 13, 1861. It was written to Secretary Chase by Rev. M.R. Watkinson, Minister of the Gospel from Ridleyville, Pennsylvania, and read:

U.S. Department of the Treasury, Fact Sheets, Currency & Coins, "History of 'In God We Trust'." www.ustreas.gov.

Dear Sir: You are about to submit your annual report to the Congress respecting the affairs of the national finances.

One fact touching our currency has hitherto been seriously overlooked. I mean the recognition of the Almighty God in some form on our coins.

You are probably a Christian. What if our Republic were not shattered beyond reconstruction [by the Civil War]? Would not the antiquaries [historians] of succeeding centuries rightly reason from our past that we were a heathen nation? What I propose is that instead of the goddess of liberty we shall have next inside the 13 stars a ring inscribed with the words PERPETUAL UNION; within the ring the allseeing eye, crowned with a halo; beneath this eye the American flag, bearing in its field stars equal to the number of the States united; in the folds of the bars the words GOD, LIBERTY, LAW.

This would make a beautiful coin, to which no possible citizen could object. This would relieve us from the ignominy of heathenism. This would place us openly under the Divine protection we have personally claimed. From my hearth I have felt our national shame in disowning God as not the least of our present national disasters.

To you first I address a subject that must be agitated.

A Motto for Coins

As a result, Secretary Chase instructed James Pollock, Director of the Mint at Philadelphia, to prepare a motto, in a letter dated November 20, 1861:

Dear Sir: No nation can be strong except in the strength of God, or safe except in His defense. The trust of our people in God should be declared on our national coins.

You will cause a device to be prepared without unnecessary delay with a motto expressing in the fewest and tersest words possible this national recognition.

It was found that the Act of Congress dated January 18, 1837, prescribed the mottoes and devices that should be placed upon the coins of the United States. This meant that the mint could make no changes without the enactment of additional legislation by the Congress. In December 1863, the Director of the Mint submitted designs for new one-cent coin, two-cent coin, and three-cent coin to Secretary Chase for approval. He proposed that upon the designs either OUR COUNTRY; OUR GOD or GOD, OUR TRUST should appear as a motto on the coins. In a letter to the Mint Director on December 9, 1863, Secretary Chase stated:

> I approve your mottoes, only suggesting that on that with the Washington obverse the motto should begin with the word OUR, so as to read OUR GOD AND OUR COUN-TRY. And on that with the shield, it should be changed so as to read: IN GOD WE TRUST.

The Congress passed the Act of April 22, 1864. This legislation changed the composition of the one-cent coin and authorized the minting of the two-cent coin. The Mint Director was directed to develop the designs for these coins for final approval of the Secretary. IN GOD WE TRUST first appeared on the 1864 two-cent coin.

Another Act of Congress passed on March 3, 1865. It allowed the Mint Director, with the Secretary's approval, to place the motto on all gold and silver coins that "shall admit the inscription thereon." Under the Act, the motto was placed on the gold double-eagle coin, the gold eagle coin, and the gold half-eagle coin. It was also placed on the silver dollar coin, the half-dollar coin and the quarter-dollar coin, and on the nickel three-cent coin beginning in 1866. Later, Congress passed the Coinage Act of February 12, 1873. It also said that the Secretary "may cause the motto IN GOD WE TRUST to be inscribed on such coins as shall admit of such motto."

The use of IN GOD WE TRUST has not been uninterrupted. The motto disappeared from the five-cent coin in

1883, and did not reappear until production of the Jefferson nickel began in 1938. Since 1938, all United States coins bear the inscription. Later, the motto was found missing from the new design of the double-eagle gold coin and the eagle gold coin shortly after they appeared in 1907. In response to a general demand, Congress ordered it restored, and the Act of May 18, 1908, made it mandatory on all coins upon which it had previously appeared. IN GOD WE TRUST was not mandatory on the one-cent coin and five-cent coin. It could be placed on them by the Secretary or the Mint Director with the Secretary's approval.

The motto has been in continuous use on the one-cent coin since 1909, and on the ten-cent coin since 1916. It also has appeared on all gold coins and silver dollar coins, half-dollar coins, and quarter-dollar coins struck since July 1, 1908.

National Motto

A law passed by the 84th Congress (P.L. 84-140) and approved by the President on July 30, 1956, the President approved a Joint Resolution of the 84th Congress, declaring IN GOD WE TRUST the national motto of the United States. IN GOD WE TRUST was first used on paper money in 1957, when it appeared on the one-dollar silver certificate. The first paper currency bearing the motto entered circulation on October 1, 1957. The Bureau of Engraving and Printing (BEP) was converting to the dry intaglio printing process. During this conversion, it gradually included IN GOD WE TRUST in the back design of all classes and denominations of currency.

As a part of a comprehensive modernization program the BEP successfully developed and installed new high-speed rotary intaglio printing presses in 1957. These allowed BEP to print currency by the dry intaglio process, 32 notes to the sheet. One-dollar silver certificates were the first denomination printed on the new high-speed presses. They included IN GOD WE TRUST as part of the reverse design as BEP adopted new dies according to the law. The motto also appeared on one-dollar silver certificates of the 1957-A and 1957-B series.

BEP prints United States paper currency by an intaglio process from engraved plates. It was necessary, therefore, to engrave the motto into the printing plates as a part of the basic engraved design to give it the prominence it deserved.

One-dollar silver certificates series 1935, 1935-A, 1935-B, 1935-C, 1935-D, 1935-E, 1935-F, 1935-G, and 1935-H were all printed on the older flat-bed presses by the wet intaglio process. P.L. 84-140 recognized that an enormous expense would be associated with immediately replacing the costly printing plates. The law allowed BEP to gradually convert to the inclusion of IN GOD WE TRUST on the currency. Accordingly, the motto is not found on series 1935-E and 1935-F one-dollar notes. By September 1961, IN GOD WE TRUST had been added to the back design of the Series 1935-G notes. Some early printings of this series do not bear the motto. IN GOD WE TRUST appears on all series 1935-H one-dollar silver certificates.

The Scopes Trial: Creationism Triumphs over Evolution

H.L. Mencken

H.L. Mencken was one of the most influential writers of his age. His satirical columns in the Baltimore Sun *and elsewhere ruthlessly attacked everything he found ignorant, hypocritical, and contemptible in American society, but in a humorous style that earned the admiration of Jazz Age icons like F. Scott Fitzgerald and Dorothy Parker. One of his favorite targets was religion, especially evangelical Christianity. In 1925, he attended the so-called Scopes Monkey Trial, in which high school teacher John Scopes was tried for violating a Tennessee law against teaching the Darwinian theory of evolution in public schools. Despite a stirring defense by famed civil rights attorney Clarence Darrow, Scopes lost, but it turned out to be a costly victory for the evangelicals. The trial attracted worldwide attention, mostly unfavorable, and columns like the following helped cement the idea of evangelical Christians as antiscientific fanatics unfit for the modern world.*

Chattanooga, Tenn., July 11.—Life down here in the Cumberland mountains realizes almost perfectly the ideal of those righteous and devoted men, [prominent Biblical literalists] Dr. Howard A. Kelly, the Rev. Dr. W.W. Davis, the Hon. Richard H. Edmonds and the Hon. Henry S. Dulaney. That is to say, evangelical Christianity is one hundred per cent triumphant. There is, of course, a certain subterranean heresy, but it is so cowed that it is almost inarticulate, and at its worst it would pass for the strictest orthodoxy in such Sodoms of infidelity as Baltimore. It may seem fabulous, but it is a sober fact that a sound Episcopalian or even a Northern Methodist

H.L. Mencken, "Mencken Likens Trial to a Religious Orgy, with a Defendant a Beelzebub," *The Baltimore Evening Sun*, July 11, 1925.

would be regarded as virtually an atheist in Dayton [Tennessee, site of the Scopes trial]. Here the only genuine conflict is between true believers. Of a given text in Holy Writ one faction may say this thing and another that, but both agree unreservedly that the text itself is impeccable [perfect], and neither in the midst of the most violent disputation [argument] would venture to accuse the other of doubt.

To call a man a doubter in these parts is equal to accusing him of cannibalism. Even the infidel Scopes himself is not charged with any such infamy. What they say of him, at worst, is that he permitted himself to be used as a cat's paw [tool] by scoundrels eager to destroy the anti-evolution law for their own dark and hellish ends. There is, it appears, a conspiracy of scientists afoot. Their purpose is to break down religion, propagate immorality, and so reduce mankind to the level of the brutes. They are the sworn and sinister agents of Beelzebub [the devil], who yearns to conquer the world, and has his eye especially upon Tennessee. Scopes is thus an agent of Beelzebub once removed, but that is as far as any fair man goes in condemning him. He is young and yet full of folly. When the secular arm has done execution upon him, the pastors will tackle him and he will be saved.

Hopelessly Biased Jury

The selection of a jury to try him, which went on all yesterday afternoon in the atmosphere of a blast furnace, showed to what extreme lengths the salvation of the local primates has been pushed. It was obvious after a few rounds that the jury would be unanimously hot for [the Creation story in the book of] Genesis. The most that Mr. [Clarence] Darrow could hope for was to sneak in a few men bold enough to declare publicly that they would have to hear the evidence against Scopes before condemning him. The slightest sign of anything further brought forth a peremptory challenge from the State. Once a man was challenged without examination for simply admitting that he did not belong formally to any church. Another time a panel man who confessed that he was prejudiced against evolution got a hearty round of applause from the crowd.

The whole process quickly took on an air of strange unreality, at least to a stranger from heathen parts. The desire of the judge to be fair to the defense, and even polite and helpful, was obvious enough—in fact, he more than once stretched the local rules of procedure in order to give Darrow a hand. But it was equally obvious that the whole thing was resolving itself into the trial of a man by his sworn enemies. A local pastor led off with a prayer calling on God to put down heresy; the judge himself charged the grand jury to protect the schools against subversive ideas. And when the candidates for the petit jury [the actual trial jury] came up Darrow had to pass fundamentalist after fundamentalist into the box—some of them glaring at him as if they expected him to go off with a sulphurous bang every time he mopped his bald head.

In brief this is a strictly Christian community, and such is its notion of fairness, justice and due process of law. Try to picture a town made up wholly of [fundamentalists] Dr. [George W.] Crabbes and Dr. Kellys, and you will have a reasonably accurate image of it. Its people are simply unable to imagine a man who rejects the literal authority of the Bible. The most they can conjure up, straining until they are red in the face, is a man who is in error about the meaning of this or that text. Thus one accused of heresy among them is like one accused of boiling his grandmother to make soap in Maryland. He must resign himself to being tried by a jury wholly innocent of any suspicion of the crime he is charged with and unanimously convinced that it is infamous. Such a jury, in the legal sense, may be fair. That is, it may be willing to hear the evidence against him before bumping him off. But it would certainly be spitting into the eye of reason to call it impartial.

A Religious Orgy

The trial, indeed, takes on, for all its legal forms, something of the air of a religious orgy. The applause of the crowd I have already mentioned. Judge Raulston rapped it down and threatened to clear the room if it was repeated, but he was quite unable to still its echoes under his very windows. The courthouse is surrounded by a large lawn, and it is peppered day and night with evangelists. One and all they are fundamentalists and their yells and bawlings fill the air with orthodoxy. I have listened to twenty of them and had private discourse with a dozen, and I have yet to find one who doubted so much as the typographical errors in Holy Writ. They dispute raucously and far into the night, but they begin and end on the common ground of complete faith. One of these holy men wears a sign on his back announcing that he is the Bible champion of the world. He told me today that he had studied the Bible four hours a day for thirty-three years, and that he had devised a plan of salvation that would save the worst sinner ever heard of, even a scientist, a theater actor or a pirate on the high seas, in forty days. This gentleman denounced the hard-shell Baptists as swindlers. He admitted freely that their sorcerers were powerful preachers and could save any ordinary man from sin, but he said that they were impotent against iniquity [evil]. The distinction is unknown to city theologians, but is as real down here as that between sanctification and salvation. The local experts, in fact, debate it daily. The Bible champion, just as I left him, was challenged by one such professor, and the two were still hard at it an hour later.

Most of the participants in such recondite combats, of course, are yokels from the hills, where no sound is heard after sundown save the roar of the catamount [mountain lion] and the wailing of departed spirits, and a man thus has time to ponder the divine mysteries. But it is an amazing thing that the more polished classes also participate actively. The professor who challenged the Bible champion was indistinguishable,

111

to the eye, from a bond salesman or city bootlegger. He had on a natty palm beach suit and a fashionable soft collar and he used excellent English. Obviously, he was one who had been through the local high school and perhaps a country college. Yet he was so far uncontaminated by infidelity that he stood in the hot sun for a whole hour debating a point that even bishops might be excused for dodging, winter as well as summer.

The Bible champion is matched and rivaled by whole herds of other metaphysicians, and all of them attract good houses [that is, full churches] and have to defend themselves against constant attack. The Seventh Day Adventists, the Campbellites, the Holy Rollers and a dozen other occult sects have field agents on the ground. They follow the traveling judges through all this country. Everywhere they go, I am told, they find the natives ready to hear them and dispute with them. They find highly accomplished theologians in every village, but even in the county towns they never encounter a genuine skeptic. If a man has doubts in this immensely pious country, he keeps them to himself.

Fundamentalism in Practice

Dr. Kelly should come down here and see his dreams made real. He will find a people who not only accept the Bible as an infallible handbook of history, geology, biology and celestial physics, but who also practice its moral precepts—at all events, up to the limit of human capacity. It would be hard to imagine a more moral town than Dayton. If it has any bootleggers, no visitor has heard of them. Ten minutes after I arrived a leading citizen offered me a drink made up half of white mule [moonshine] and half of coca cola, but he seems to have been simply indulging himself in a naughty gesture. No fancy woman has been seen in the town since the end of the [President William] McKinley administration. There is no gambling. There is no place to dance. The relatively wicked, when they would indulge themselves, go to Robinson's drug store and debate theology.

In a word, the new Jerusalem, the ideal of all soul savers and sin exterminators. Nine churches are scarcely enough for the 1,800 inhabitants: many of them go into the hills to shout and roll. A clergyman has the rank and authority of a major-general of artillery. A Sunday-school superintendent is believed to have the gift of prophecy. But what of life here? Is it more agreeable than in Babylon? I regret that I must have to report that it is not. The incessant clashing of theologians grows monotonous in a day and intolerable the day following. One longs for a merry laugh, a burst of happy music, the gurgle of a decent jug [of liquor]. Try a meal in the hotel; it is tasteless and swims in grease. Go to the drug store and call for refreshment: the boy will hand you almost automatically a beaker of coca cola. Look at the magazine counter: a pile of *Saturday Evening Posts* two feet high. Examine the books: melodrama and cheap amour. Talk to a town magnifico [prominent person]; he knows nothing that is not in Genesis.

I propose that Dr. Kelly be sent here for sixty days, preferably in the heat of summer. He will return to Baltimore yelling for a carboy [large glass bottle] of pilsner and eager to master the saxophone [considered a diabolical instrument]. His soul perhaps will be lost, but he will be a merry and a happy man.

THE HISTORY OF ISSUES

CHAPTER 4

The Wall of Separation and Its Opponents

Chapter Preface

Even moreso than in the preceding centuries in the United States, the twentieth century would see religiously based strife at the federal level, particularly in the courts. In addition, the role of religion itself, as opposed to tolerance for particular religions, would become more of an issue.

At first, this seemed unlikely. The success of the abolition of slavery, and later the prohibition of alcohol, seemed to confirm the power of religious groups and individuals to shape public policy. So did the success of the so-called social gospel. This was a movement within liberal Protestantism that called for much more social activism on the part of Christians, including private charities, public agitation for universal education, shorter workdays, and the abolition of child labor. At the same time, many clearly religious public policies, such as prayer in schools and laws that closed businesses on Sundays, remained widespread and uncontroversial.

Some developments at the federal level would change this situation, however, beginning with the constitutional doctrine of incorporation. In *Gitlow v. New York* in 1925, the U.S. Supreme Court ruled that the free speech rights guaranteed by the First Amendment applied to the states as well as the federal government, because of the due process clause of the Fourteenth Amendment. Gradually more and more of the Bill of Rights' guarantees have been "incorporated" into state legislation, giving the federal courts influence over more and more state and local government decision making. This is what gave the Supreme Court the power to strike down prayer in schools and to guarantee abortion rights. In turn, these two decisions inspired the rebirth of the Religious Right, which has dramatically reshaped debates over church and state.

Also, beginning with the New Deal of the 1930s, there was an expanded role for the federal government in many areas of life. At first, these concerned things such as bringing electricity to rural areas, building a national highway system, and instituting Social Security, none of which had any obvious connection to anybody's religious beliefs (although even here some feared that the assigning of Social Security numbers was a sign that the antichrist of the Book of Revelation was a step nearer). However, a growing federal role in areas such as education and health care did create some more obviously religious tensions. One example is the argument over whether the federal government should support stem cell research, which arose in the first year of the George W. Bush administration. In previous eras, the federal government would not have been called upon to take any position at all on this difficult religious question. Similarly, questions about whether taxpayers should fund abortions, accredit colleges that reject the teaching of evolution, or allow a hospital to disconnect the life support of an apparently brain dead woman, have become national questions where before they might have been purely local, if not completely private and outside politics.

Together, this growing influence of the Supreme Court and the federal government as a whole have put religion itself into the realm of national politics. It is no longer acceptable to say that Alabama can have school prayer and California cannot. It is necessary to decide for both. It is still possible to decide that the federal government can refuse to fund something without outlawing it, but in some areas of scientific research (such as stem cell research), refusing to fund can severely inhibit and delay the research itself. So it often appears that presidents, congressional leaders, and Supreme Court justices are making seemingly theological decisions.

In turn, secularists and atheists have been taking a much more public and prominent role in the national debate. In the past, atheists have been marginalized as dangerous subversives, as un-American Communists, and as people who have no place in any discussion of morality. There have always been individuals who have rejected these characterizations, but to-day as never before more Americans are coming out clearly as atheists. In June 2007 the Barna Group, a leading surveyor of religious attitudes, found that approximately one in eleven Americans considered themselves either atheist or agnostic, re-jecting a belief in any Supreme Being. Significantly, more than one in four Americans between the ages of eighteen and twenty-two considered themselves to be in this category.

These changes are dramatic, but they may obscure an even more dramatic truth. In other developed countries, atheists are a much larger percentage. Only 52 percent of citizens in European Union nations say they believe there is a God, a number including only 32 percent of Czechs, 23 percent of Swedes, and 16 percent of Estonians. Clearly, religion is flour-ishing in the United States compared with many of the na-tions from which many Americans or their forebears emi-grated.

For some, this is proof that the ideal of separation of church and state is good for both religion and democracy. For others, it is an indication that religion deserves more respect in American politics. For the society as a whole, it is a chal-lenge that will continue well into the current century.

There Must Be a Wall of Separation Between Church and State

Hugo Black

The phrase "a wall of separation" appears in a letter written by Thomas Jefferson, but it was Hugo Black who made it such a common phrase in questions of church and state. By quoting Jefferson in the majority opinion for Everson v. Board of Education, *Justice Black created a strong image embraced by advocates of keeping government and religion out of each other's affairs. At the same time, the* Everson *decision itself upheld New Jersey's legislation allowing local governments to reimburse the parents of Catholic parochial school students for the costs of busing those students. Clearly, some amount of interaction between church and state was allowed. For the 5-4 majority, the issue came down to whether the support was primarily neutral. Just as towns could provide police and fire protection to religious schools, and indeed churches and synagogues, they could provide help for all parents who chose to send their children to school on a public bus, whether the school was religious or not. As Justice Black explained, government was not supposed to help any particular religion, or religion itself; however, it was not supposed to hinder it either, such as by withholding commonly available public services that had no religious purpose.*

Born in 1886, Hugo Black was a Democratic senator and a close ally of Franklin Delano Roosevelt when he was appointed to the Court in 1937. He emerged as one of the most influential justices in history, especially through his strong support for incorporation, the judicial doctrine that the Bill of Rights limits state governments as well as the federal government. He is also known for his support of a literalist reading of Constitutional rights,

Hugo Black, majority opinion, *Everson v. Board of Education of Ewing TP.*, 330 U.S. 1 (1947).

which made him difficult to define as a liberal or conservative on the Court. He died in 1971 approximately a month after retiring from the Court.

A New Jersey statute authorizes its local school districts to make rules and contracts for the transportation of children to and from schools. The appellee, a township board of education, acting pursuant to this statute authorized reimbursement to parents of money expended by them for the bus transportation of their children on regular busses operated by the public transportation system. Part of this money was for the payment of transportation of some children in the community to Catholic parochial schools. These church schools give their students, in addition to secular education, regular religious instruction conforming to the religious tenets [beliefs] and modes of worship of the Catholic Faith. The superintendent of these schools is a Catholic priest.

The appellant, in his capacity as a district taxpayer, filed suit in a State court challenging the right of the Board to reimburse parents of parochial school students. He contended that the statute and the resolution passed pursuant to it violated both the State and the Federal Constitutions. That court held that the legislature was without power to authorize such payment under the State constitution. The New Jersey Court of Errors and Appeals reversed, holding that neither the statute nor the resolution passed pursuant to it was in conflict with the State constitution or the provisions of the Federal Constitution in issue. The case is here on appeal.

Since there has been no attack on the statute on the ground that a part of its language excludes children attending private schools operated for profit from enjoying state payment for their transportation, we need not consider this exclusionary language; it has no relevancy to any constitutional question here presented. Furthermore, if the exclusion clause had been properly challenged, we do not know whether New Jersey's highest court would construe its statutes as precluding payment of the school transportation of any group of pupils, even those of a private school run for profit. Consequently, we put to one side the question as to the validity of the statute against the claim that it does not authorize payment for the transportation generally of school children in New Jersey.

Constitutional Objections

The only contention here is that the State statute and the resolution, in so far as they authorized reimbursement to parents of children attending parochial schools, violate the Federal Constitution in these two respects, which to some extent, overlap. First. They authorize the State to take by taxation the private property of some and bestow it upon others, to be used for their own private purposes. This, it is alleged, violates the due process clause of the Fourteenth Amendment. Second. The statute and the resolution forced inhabitants to pay taxes to help support and maintain schools which are dedicated to, and which regularly teach, the Catholic Faith. This is alleged to be a use of State power to support church schools contrary to the prohibition of the First Amendment which the Fourteenth Amendment made applicable to the states.

First. The due process argument that the State law taxes some people to help others carry out their private purposes is framed in two phases. The first phase is that a state cannot tax A to reimburse B for the cost of transporting his children to church schools. This is said to violate the due process clause because the children are sent to these church schools to satisfy the personal desires of their parents, rather than the public's interest in the general education of all children. This argument, if valid, would apply equally to prohibit state payment for the transportation of children to any non-public school, whether operated by a church, or any other nongovernment individual or group. But, the New Jersey legislature has decided that a public purpose will be served by using tax-raised funds to pay the bus fares of all school children, including those who attend parochial schools. The New Jersey Court of Errors and Appeals has reached the same conclusion. The fact that a state law, passed to satisfy a public need, coincides with the personal desires of the individuals most directly affected is certainly an inadequate reason for us to say that a legislature has erroneously appraised the public need.

It is true that this Court has, in rare instances, struck down state statutes on the ground that the purpose for which tax-raised funds were to be expended was not a public one. . . . But the Court has also pointed out that this far-reaching authority must be exercised with the most extreme caution. Otherwise, a state's power to legislate for the public welfare might be seriously curtailed, a power which is a primary reason for the existence of states. Changing local conditions create new local problems which may lead a state's people and its local authorities to believe that laws authorizing new types of public services are necessary to promote the general well-being of the people. The Fourteenth Amendment did not strip the states of their power to meet problems previously left for individual solution. . . .

It is much too late to argue that legislation intended to facilitate the opportunity of children to get a secular education serves no public purpose. The same thing is no less true of legislation to reimburse needy parents, or all parents, for payment of the fares of their children so that they can ride in public busses to and from schools rather than run the risk of traffic and other hazards incident to walking or 'hitchhiking'. . . Nor does it follow that a law has a private rather than a public purpose because it provides that tax-raised funds will be paid to reimburse individuals on account of money spent by them in a way which furthers a public program. Subsidies and loans to individuals such as farmers and home owners, and to privately owned transportation systems, as well as many other kinds of businesses, have been commonplace practices in our state and national history.

Question of Establishment Clause

Insofar as the second phase of the due process argument may differ from the first, it is by suggesting that taxation for transportation of children to church schools constitutes support of a religion by the State. But if the law is invalid for this reason, it is because it violates the First Amendment's prohibition against the establishment of religion by law. This is the exact question raised by appellant's second contention, to consideration of which we now turn.

Second. The New Jersey statute is challenged as a 'law respecting an establishment of religion.' The First Amendment, as made applicable to the states by the Fourteenth, *Murdock v. Commonwealth of Pennsylvania*, commands that a state 'shall make no law respecting an establishment of religion, or prohibiting the free exercise thereof.' These words of the First Amendment reflected in the minds of early Americans a vivid mental picture of conditions and practices which they fervently wished to stamp out in order to preserve liberty for themselves and for their posterity. Doubtless their goal has not been entirely reached; but so far has the Nation moved toward it that the expression 'law respecting an establishment of religion,' probably does not so vividly remind present-day Americans of the evils, fears, and political problems that caused that expression to be written into our Bill of Rights. Whether this New Jersey law is one respecting the 'establishment of religion' requires an understanding of the meaning of that language, particularly with respect to the imposition of taxes. Once again, therefore, it is not inappropriate briefly to review the background and environment of the period in which that constitutional language was fashioned and adopted.

A large proportion of the early settlers of this country came here from Europe to escape the bondage of laws which compelled them to support and attend government-favored churches. The centuries immediately before and contemporaneous with the colonization of America had been filled with turmoil, civil strife, and persecutions, generated in large part by established sects determined to maintain their absolute political and religious supremacy. With the power of government supporting them, at various times and places, Catholics had persecuted Protestants, Protestants had persecuted Catholics, Protestant sects had persecuted other Protestant sects, Catholics of one shade of belief had persecuted Catholics of another shade of belief, and all of these had from time to time persecuted Jews. In efforts to force loyalty to whatever religious group happened to be on top and in league with the government of a particular time and place, men and women had been fined, cast in jail, cruelly tortured, and killed. Among the offenses for which these punishments had been inflicted were such things as speaking disrespectfully of the views of ministers of government-established churches, nonattendance at those churches, expressions of non-belief in their doctrines, and failure to pay taxes and tithes to support them.

A Reaction to Oppression

These practices of the old world were transplanted to and began to thrive in the soil of the new America. The very charters granted by the English Crown to the individuals and companies designated to make the laws which would control the destinies of the colonials authorized these individuals and companies to erect religious establishments which all, whether believers or non-believers, would be required to support and attend. An exercise of this authority was accompanied by a repetition of many of the old-world practices and persecutions. Catholics found themselves hounded and proscribed because of their faith; Quakers who followed their conscience went to jail; Baptists were peculiarly obnoxious to certain dominant Protestant sects; men and women of varied faiths who happened to be in a minority in a particular locality were persecuted because they steadfastly persisted in worshipping God only as their own consciences dictated. And all of these dissenters were compelled to pay tithes and taxes to support government-sponsored churches whose ministers preached inflammatory sermons designed to strengthen and consolidate the established faith by generating a burning hatred against dissenters. These practices became so commonplace as to shock the freedom-loving colonials into a feeling of abhorrence. The imposition of taxes to pay ministers' salaries and to build and maintain churches and church property aroused their indignation. It was these feelings which found expression in the First Amendment. No one locality and no one group throughout the Colonies can rightly be given entire credit for having aroused the sentiment that culminated in adoption of the Bill of Rights' provisions embracing religious liberty. But Virginia, where the established church had achieved a dominant influence in political affairs and where many excesses attracted wide public attention, provided a great stimulus and able leadership for the movement. The people there, as elsewhere, reached the conviction that individual religious liberty could be achieved best under a government which was stripped of all power to tax, to support, or otherwise to assist any or all religions, or to interfere with the beliefs of any religious individual or group.

The movement toward this end reached its dramatic climax in Virginia in 1785–86 when the Virginia legislative body was about to renew Virginia's tax levy for the support of the established church. Thomas Jefferson and James Madison led the fight against this tax. Madison wrote his great Memorial and Remonstrance against the law. In it, he eloquently argued that a true religion did not need the support of law; that no person, either believer or non-believer, should be taxed to support a religious institution of any kind; that the best interest of a society required that the minds of men always be wholly free; and that cruel persecutions were the inevitable result of government-established religions. Madison's Remonstrance received strong support throughout Virginia, and the

Assembly postponed consideration of the proposed tax measure until its next session. When the proposal came up for consideration at that session, it not only died in committee, but the Assembly enacted the famous 'Virginia Bill for Religious Liberty' originally written by Thomas Jefferson. The preamble to that Bill stated among other things that

> 'Almighty God hath created the mind free; that all attempts to influence it by temporal punishments, or burthens [burdens], or by civil incapacitations, tend only to beget habits of hypocrisy and meanness, and are a departure from the plan of the Holy author of our religion who being Lord both of body and mind, yet chose not to propagate it by coercions on either . . .; that to compel a man to furnish contributions of money for the propagation of opinions which he disbelieves, is sinful and tyrannical; that even the forcing him to support this or that teacher of his own religious persuasion, is depriving him of the comfortable liberty of giving his contributions to the particular pastor, whose morals he would make his pattern . . . '

And the statute itself enacted

> That no man shall be compelled to frequent or support any religious worship, place, or ministry whatsoever, nor shall be enforced, restrained, molested, or burthened, in his body or goods, nor shall otherwise suffer on account of his religious opinions or belief. . . .

Applying the First Amendment

This Court has previously recognized that the provisions of the First Amendment, in the drafting and adoption of which Madison and Jefferson played such leading roles, had the same objective and were intended to provide the same protection against governmental intrusion on religious liberty as the Virginia statute. Prior to the adoption of the Fourteenth Amendment, the First Amendment did not apply as a restraint against the states. Most of them did soon provide similar constitutional protections for religious liberty. But some states persisted for about half a century in imposing restraints upon the free exercise of religion and in discriminating against particular religious groups. In recent years, so far as the provision against the establishment of a religion is concerned, the question has most frequently arisen in connection with proposed state aid to church schools and efforts to carry on religious teachings in the public schools in accordance with the tenets of a particular sect. Some churches have either sought or accepted state financial support for their schools. Here again the efforts to obtain state aid or acceptance of it have not been limited to any one particular faith. The state courts, in the main, have remained faithful to the language of their own constitutional provisions designed to protect religious freedom and to separate religious and governments. Their decisions, however, show the difficulty in drawing the line between tax legislation which provides funds for the welfare of the general public and that which is designed to support institutions which teach religion.

The meaning and scope of the First Amendment, preventing establishment of religion or prohibiting the free exercise thereof, in the light of its history and the evils it was designed forever to suppress, have been several times elaborated by the decisions of this Court prior to the application of the First Amendment to the states by the Fourteenth. The broad meaning given the Amendment by these earlier cases has been accepted by this Court in its decisions concerning an individual's religious freedom rendered since the Fourteenth Amendment was interpreted to make the prohibitions of the First applicable to state action abridging religious freedom. There is every reason to give the same application and broad interpretation to the 'establishment of religion' clause. The interrelation of these complementary clauses was well summarized in a statement of the Court of Appeals of South Carolina, quoted with approval by this Court, in *Watson v. Jones*. 'The structure of our government has, for the preservation of civil liberty, rescued the temporal institutions from religious interference. On the other hand, it has secured religious liberty from the invasions of the civil authority.'

Wall of Separation

The 'establishment of religion' clause of the First Amendment means at least this: Neither a state nor the Federal Government can set up a church. Neither can pass laws which aid one religion, aid all religions, or prefer one religion over another. Neither can force nor influence a person to go to or to remain away from church against his will or force him to profess a belief or disbelief in any religion. No person can be punished for entertaining or professing religious beliefs or disbeliefs, for church attendance or non-attendance. No tax in any amount, large or small, can be levied to support any religious activities or institutions, whatever they may be called, or whatever form they may adopt to teach or practice religion. Neither a state nor the Federal Government can, openly or secretly, participate in the affairs of any religious organizations or groups and vice versa. In the words of Jefferson, the clause against establishment of religion by law was intended to erect 'a wall of separation between Church and State.' *Reynolds v. United States.*

We must consider the New Jersey statute in accordance with the foregoing limitations imposed by the First Amendment. But we must not strike that state statute down if it is within the state's constitutional power even though it approaches the verge of that power. New Jersey cannot consistently with the 'establishment of religion' clause of the First Amendment contribute tax-raised funds to the support of an institution which teaches the tenets and faith of any church. On the other hand, other language of the amendment commands that New Jersey cannot hamper its citizens in the free exercise of their own religion. Consequently, it cannot exclude individual Catholics, Lutherans, Mohammedans, Baptists, Jews, Methodists, Non-believers, Presbyterians, or the members of any other faith, because of their faith, or lack of it, from receiving the benefits of public welfare legislation. While we do not mean to intimate that a state could not provide transportation only to children attending public schools, we must be careful, in protecting the citizens of New Jersey against state-established churches, to be sure that we do not inadvertently prohibit New Jersey from extending its general State law benefits to all its citizens without regard to their religious belief Measured by these standards, we cannot say that the First Amendment prohibits New Jersey from spending tax-raised funds to pay the bus fares of parochial school pupils as a part of a general program under which it pays the fares of pupils attending public and other schools. It is undoubtedly true that children are helped to get to church schools. There is even a possibility that some of the children might not be sent to the church schools if the parents were compelled to pay their children's bus fares out of their own pockets when transportation to a public school would have been paid for by the State. The same possibility exists where the state requires a local transit company to provide reduced fares to school children including those attending parochial schools, or where a municipally owned transportation system undertakes to carry all school children free of charge. Moreover, state-paid policemen, detailed to protect children going to and from church schools from the very real hazards of traffic, would serve much the same purpose and accomplish much the same result as state provisions intended to guarantee free transportation of a kind which the state deems to be best for the school children's welfare. And parents might refuse to risk their children to the serious danger of traffic accidents going to and from parochial schools, the approaches to which were not protected by policemen. Similarly, parents might be reluctant to permit their children to attend schools which the state had cut off from such general government services as ordinary police and fire protection, connections for sewage disposal, public highways and sidewalks. Of course, cutting off church schools from these services, so separate and so indisputably marked off from the religious function, would make it far more difficult for the schools to operate. But such is obviously not the purpose of the First Amendment. That Amendment requires the state to be a neutral [party] in its relations with groups of religious believers and non-believers; it does not require the state to be their adversary. State power is no more to be used so as to handicap religions, than it is to favor them.

This Court has said that parents may, in the discharge of their duty under state compulsory education laws, send their children to a religious rather than a public school if the school meets the secular educational requirements which the state has power to impose. It appears that these parochial schools meet New Jersey's requirements. The State contributes no money to the schools. It does not support them. Its legislation, as applied, does no more than provide a general program to help parents get their children, regardless of their religion, safely and expeditiously to and from accredited schools.

The First Amendment has erected a wall between church and state. That wall must be kept high and impregnable. We could not approve the slightest breach. New Jersey has not breached it here.

American Leaders Do Not Answer to Religious Organizations

John F. Kennedy

Hoping to become the nation's first Catholic president, John F. Kennedy had to overcome a deeply ingrained prejudice. Many Protestants feared that his religion would require him to answer to the pope or to the bishops of his church. A little more than a month before the 1960 presidential election, Kennedy decided to address these concerns directly in a speech to Southern Baptist ministers in Houston, Texas. He emphasized that he was not the "Catholic" nominee, but the Democratic nominee who happened to be a Catholic. He emphasized even more strongly that he believed in the separation of church and state and would never undermine the First Amendment or in any way feel bound by the opinion of any religious leader. Finally, he called for an end to the kind of religious intolerance that would single out any sect as unfit for the presidency. The speech was well-received, although anti-Catholicism continued to play at least some role in the rest of the campaign. Nevertheless, this particular religious test has all but evaporated since Kennedy's election, and his speech stands as a testament to the ideals of religious tolerance and the separation of church and state.

I am grateful for your generous invitation to state my views.

While the so-called religious issue is necessarily and properly the chief topic here tonight, I want to emphasize from the outset that I believe that we have far more critical issues in the 1960 election: the spread of Communist influence, until it now festers only ninety miles off the coast of Florida—the hu-

John F. Kennedy, "Address to Southern Baptist Leaders," 1960.

miliating treatment of our President and Vice President by those who no longer respect our power—the hungry children I saw in West Virginia, the old people who cannot pay their doctor's bills, the families forced to give up their farms—an America with too many slums, with too few schools, and too late to the moon and outer space.

These are the real issues which should decide this campaign. And they are not religious issues—for war and hunger and ignorance and despair know no religious barrier.

But because I am a Catholic and no Catholic has ever been elected President, the real issues in this campaign have been obscured—perhaps deliberately, in some quarters less responsible than this. So it is apparently necessary for me to state once again—not what kind of church I believe in, for that should be important only to me, but what kind of America I believe in.

Absolute Separation of Church and State

I believe in an America where the separation of church and state is absolute—where no Catholic prelate would tell the President (should he be a Catholic) how to act and no Protestant minister would tell his parishioners for whom to vote— where no church or church school is granted any public funds or political preference—and where no man is denied public office merely because his religion differs from the President who might appoint him or the people who might elect him.

I believe in an America that is officially neither Catholic, Protestant nor Jewish—where no public official either requests or accepts instructions on public policy from the Pope, the National Council of Churches or any other ecclesiastical source—where no religious body seeks to impose its will directly or indirectly upon the general populace or the public acts of its officials—and where religious liberty is so indivisible that an act against one church is treated as an act against all.

For, while this year it may be a Catholic against whom the finger of suspicion is pointed, in other years it has been, and may someday be again, a Jew—or a Quaker—or a Unitarian—or a Baptist. It was Virginia's harassment of Baptist preachers, for example, that led to Jefferson's statute of religious freedom. Today, I may be the victim—but tomorrow it may be you—until the whole fabric of our harmonious society is ripped apart at a time of great national peril.

Finally, I believe in an America where religious intolerance will someday end—where all men and all churches are treated as equal—where every man has the same right to attend or not to attend the church of his choice—where there is no Catholic vote, no anti-Catholic vote, no bloc voting of any kind—and where Catholics, Protestants and Jews, both the lay and the pastoral level, will refrain from those attitudes of disdain and division which have so often marred their works in the past, and promote instead the American ideal of brotherhood.

Religion Is a Private Affair

That is the kind of America in which I believe. And it represents the kind of Presidency in which I believe—a great office that must be neither humbled by making it the instrument of any religious group, nor tarnished by arbitrarily withholding its occupancy from the members of any religious group. I believe in a President whose views on religion are his own private affair, neither imposed upon him by the nation or imposed by the nation upon him as a condition to holding that office.

I would not look with favor upon a President working to subvert the First Amendment's guarantees of religious liberty (nor would our system of checks and balances permit him to do so). And neither do I look with favor upon those who would work to subvert Article VI of the Constitution by requiring a religious test—even by indirection—for if they disagree with that safeguard, they should be openly working to repeal it.

I want a chief executive whose public acts are responsible to all and obligated to none—who can attend any ceremony, service or dinner his office may appropriately require him to fulfill—and whose fulfillment of his Presidential office is not limited or conditioned by any religious oath, ritual or obligation.

This is the kind of America I believe in—and this is the kind of America I fought for in the South Pacific and the kind my brother died for in Europe. No one suggested then that we might have a "divided loyalty," that we did "not believe in liberty" or that we belonged to a disloyal group that threatened "the freedoms for which our forefathers died."

No Religious Test

And in fact this is the kind of America for which our forefathers did die when they fled here to escape religious test oaths, that denied office to members of less favored churches, when they fought for the Constitution, the Bill of Rights, the Virginia Statute of Religious Freedom—and when they fought at the shrine I visited today—the Alamo. For side by side with Bowie and Crockett died Fuentes and McCafferty and Bailey and Bedillio and Carey—but no one knows whether they were Catholics or not. For there was no religious test there.

I ask you tonight to follow in that tradition, to judge me on the basis of fourteen years in the Congress—on my declared stands against an ambassador to the Vatican, against unconstitutional aid to parochial schools, and against any boycott of the public schools (which I attended myself)—and instead of doing this do not judge me on the basis of these pamphlets and publications we have all seen that carefully select quotations out of context from the statements of Catholic Church leaders, usually in other countries, frequently in other centuries, and rarely relevant to any situation here—and always omitting of course, that statement of the American bishops in 1948 which strongly endorsed church-state separation.

I do not consider these other quotations binding upon my public acts—why should you? But let me say, with respect to other countries, that I am wholly opposed to the state being used by any religious group, Catholic or Protestant, to compel, prohibit or prosecute the free exercise of any other religion. And that goes for any persecution at any time, by anyone, in any country.

And I hope that you and I condemn with equal fervor those nations which deny it to Catholics. And rather than cite the misdeeds of those who differ, I would also cite the record of the Catholic Church in such nations as France and Ireland—and the independence of such statesmen as [French president Charles] de Gaulle and [German chancellor Konrad] Adenauer.

But let me stress again that these are my views—for, contrary to common newspaper usage, I am not the Catholic candidate for President [but the candidate] who happens also to be a Catholic.

I do not speak for my church on public matters—and the church does not speak for me.

Role of Conscience

Whatever issue may come before me as President, if I should be elected—on birth control, divorce, censorship, gambling, or any other subject—I will make my decision in accordance with these views, in accordance with what my conscience tells me to be in the national interest, and without regard to outside religious pressure or dictate. And no power or threat of punishment could cause me to decide otherwise.

But if the time should ever come—and I do not concede any conflict to be remotely possible—when my office would require me to either violate my conscience, or violate the national interest, then I would resign the office, and I hope any other conscientious public servant would do likewise.

But I do not intend to apologize for these views to my critics of either Catholic or Protestant faith, nor do I intend to disavow either my views or my church in order to win this election. If I should lose on the real issues, I shall return to my seat in the Senate satisfied that I tried my best and was fairly judged.

But if this election is decided on the basis that 40,000,000 Americans lost their chance of being President on the day they were baptized, then it is the whole nation that will be the loser in the eyes of Catholics and non-Catholics around the world, in the eyes of history, and in the eyes of our own people.

But if, on the other hand, I should win this election, I shall devote every effort of mind and spirit to fulfilling the oath of the Presidency—practically identical, I might add with the oath I have taken for fourteen years in the Congress. For, without reservation, I can, and I quote "solemnly swear that I will faithfully execute the office of President of the United States and will preserve, protect, and defend the Constitution so help me God."

Overt Support for Religion Is Unconstitutional

Warren Burger

The Supreme Court mandated a wall of separation between church and state in 1947, in Everson v. Board of Education. *However, that same decision allowed some use of public funds for students of religious schools, which raised the question of how much public support was too much. In* Lemon v. Kurtzman, *the Court created a three-pronged test to try to answer that question. To be constitutional, the Court decided, government policy must first have a legitimate secular purpose. Second, the government's actions must not have the primary effect of helping or hindering religion. Finally, the government's action must not lead to excessive entanglement with religion. Each of these tests raises difficult questions of its own, and courts have not always been consistent in applying these tests. However, they do set somewhat clearer limits to what government can do when religion is involved.*

The author of the opinion was Warren Burger, who was appointed chief justice of the United States by President Richard Nixon in 1969, after a lengthy career as a lawyer, government official, and judge. He presided over many important decisions on desegregation, capital punishment, and abortion. He retired in 1986 and died in 1995.

These two appeals raise questions as to Pennsylvania and Rhode Island statutes providing state aid to church-related elementary and secondary schools. Both statutes are challenged as violative of the Establishment and Free Exercise Clauses of the First Amendment and the Due Process Clause of the Fourteenth Amendment.

Pennsylvania has adopted a statutory program that provides financial support to nonpublic elementary and second-

Warren Burger, majority opinion, *Lemon v. Kurtzman*, 403 U.S. 602 (1971).

ary schools by way of reimbursement for the cost of teachers' salaries, textbooks, and instructional materials in specified secular subjects. Rhode Island has adopted a statute under which the State pays directly to teachers in nonpublic elementary schools a supplement of 15% of their annual salary. Under each statute, state aid has been given to church-related educational institutions. We hold that both statutes are unconstitutional.

The Rhode Island Statute

The Rhode Island Salary Supplement Act was enacted in 1969. It rests on the legislative finding that the quality of education available in nonpublic elementary schools has been jeopardized by the rapidly rising salaries needed to attract competent and dedicated teachers. The Act authorizes state officials to supplement the salaries of teachers of secular subjects in nonpublic elementary schools by paying directly to a teacher an amount not in excess of 15% of his current annual salary. As supplemented, however, a nonpublic school teacher's salary cannot exceed the maximum paid to teachers in the State's public schools, and the recipient must be certified by the state board of education in substantially the same manner as public school teachers.

In order to be eligible for the Rhode Island salary supplement, the recipient must teach in a nonpublic school at which the average per-pupil expenditure on secular education is less than the average in the State's public schools during a specified period. Appellant State Commissioner of Education also requires eligible schools to submit financial data. If this information indicates a per-pupil expenditure in excess of the statutory limitation, the records of the school in question must be examined in order to assess how much of the expenditure is attributable to secular education and how much to religious activity.

The Act also requires that teachers eligible for salary supplements must teach only those subjects that are offered in the State's public schools. They must use "only teaching materials which are used in the public schools." Finally, any teacher applying for a salary supplement must first agree in writing "not to teach a course in religion for so long as or during such time as he or she receives any salary supplements" under the Act.

Appellees are citizens and taxpayers of Rhode Island. They brought this suit to have the Rhode Island Salary Supplement Act declared unconstitutional and its operation enjoined on the ground that it violates the Establishment and Free Exercise Clauses of the First Amendment. Appellants are state officials charged with administration of the Act, teachers eligible for salary supplements under the Act, and parents of children in church-related elementary schools whose teachers would receive state salary assistance. . . .

The District Court concluded that the Act violated the Establishment Clause, holding that it fostered "excessive entanglement" between government and religion. In addition, two judges thought that the Act had the impermissible effect of giving "significant aid to a religious enterprise." We affirm.

The Pennsylvania Statute

Pennsylvania has adopted a program that has some but not all of the features of the Rhode Island program. The Pennsylvania Nonpublic Elementary and Secondary Education Act was passed in 1968 in response to a crisis that the Pennsylvania Legislature found existed in the State's nonpublic schools due to rapidly rising costs. The statute affirmatively reflects the legislative conclusion that the State's educational goals could appropriately be fulfilled by government support of "those purely secular educational objectives achieved through nonpublic education. . . ."

The statute authorizes appellee state Superintendent of Public Instruction to "purchase" specified "secular educational services" from nonpublic schools. Under the "contracts" authorized by the statute, the State directly reimburses nonpublic schools solely for their actual expenditures for teachers' salaries, textbooks, and instructional materials. A school seeking reimbursement must maintain prescribed accounting procedures that identify the "separate" cost of the "secular educational service." These accounts are subject to state audit. The funds for this program were originally derived from a new tax on horse and harness racing, but the Act is now financed by a portion of the state tax on cigarettes.

There are several significant statutory restrictions on state aid. Reimbursement is limited to courses "presented in the curricula of the public schools." It is further limited "solely" to courses in the following "secular" subjects: mathematics, modern foreign languages, physical science, and physical education. Textbooks and instructional materials included in the program must be approved by the state Superintendent of Public Instruction. Finally, the statute prohibits reimbursement for any course that contains "any subject matter expressing religious teaching, or the morals or forms of worship of any sect."

The Act went into effect on July 1, 1968, and the first reimbursement payments to schools were made on September 2, 1969. It appears that some $5 million has been expended annually under the Act. The State has now entered into contracts with some 1,181 nonpublic elementary and secondary schools with a student population of some 535,215 pupils—more than 20% of the total number of students in the State. More than 96% of these pupils attend church-related schools, and most of these schools are affiliated with the Roman Catholic church.

Appellants brought this action in the District Court to challenge the constitutionality of the Pennsylvania statute. The organizational plaintiffs-appellants are associations of persons resident in Pennsylvania declaring belief in the separation of church and state; individual plaintiffs-appellants are citizens and taxpayers of Pennsylvania. Appellant Lemon, in addition to being a citizen and a taxpayer, is a parent of a child attending public school in Pennsylvania. Lemon also alleges that he purchased a ticket at a race track, and thus had paid the specific tax that supports the expenditures under the Act. Appellees are state officials who have the responsibility for administering the Act. In addition seven church-related schools are defendants appellees. . . .

The court granted appellees' motion to dismiss the complaint for failure to state a claim for relief. It held that the Act violated neither the Establishment nor the Free Exercise Clause, Chief Judge [William H.] Hastie dissenting. We reverse.

Everson

In *Everson v. Board of Education*, (1947), this Court upheld a state statute that reimbursed the parents of parochial school children for bus transportation expenses. There, MR. JUSTICE [HUGO] BLACK, writing for the majority, suggested that the decision carried to "the verge" of forbidden territory under the Religion Clauses. Candor [honesty] compels acknowledgment, moreover, that we can only dimly perceive the lines of demarcation in this extraordinarily sensitive area of constitutional law.

The language of the Religion Clauses of the First Amendment is at best opaque [unclear], particularly when compared with other portions of the Amendment. Its authors did not simply prohibit the establishment of a state church or a state religion, an area history shows they regarded as very important and fraught with great dangers. Instead they commanded that there should be "no law respecting an establishment of religion." A law may be one "respecting" the forbidden objective while falling short of its total realization. A law "respecting" the proscribed result, that is, the establishment of religion, is not always easily identifiable as one violative of the Clause. A given law might not establish a state religion but nevertheless be one "respecting" that end in the sense of being a step that could lead to such establishment and hence offend the First Amendment.

In the absence of precisely stated constitutional prohibitions, we must draw lines with reference to the three main evils against which the Establishment Clause was intended to afford protection: "sponsorship, financial support, and active involvement of the sovereign in religious activity." *Walz v. Tax Commission*, (1970).

Tests

Every analysis in this area must begin with consideration of the cumulative criteria developed by the Court over many years. Three such tests may be gleaned from our cases. First, the statute must have a secular legislative purpose; second, its principal or primary effect must be one that neither advances nor inhibits religion, *Board of Education v. Allen*, (1968); finally, the statute must not foster "an excessive government entanglement with religion" (*Walz*).

Inquiry into the legislative purposes of the Pennsylvania and Rhode Island statutes affords no basis for a conclusion that the legislative intent was to advance religion. On the contrary, the statutes themselves clearly state that they are intended to enhance the quality of the secular education in all schools covered by the compulsory attendance laws. There is no reason to believe the legislatures meant anything else. A State always has a legitimate concern for maintaining minimum standards in all schools it allows to operate. As in *Allen*, we find nothing here that undermines the stated legislative intent; it must therefore be accorded appropriate deference.

In *Allen* the Court acknowledged that secular and religious teachings were not necessarily so intertwined that secular textbooks furnished to students by the State were in fact instrumental in the teaching of religion. The legislatures of Rhode Island and Pennsylvania have concluded that secular and religious education are identifiable and separable. In the abstract we have no quarrel with this conclusion.

The two legislatures, however, have also recognized that church-related elementary and secondary schools have a significant religious mission and that a substantial portion of their activities is religiously oriented. They have therefore sought to create statutory restrictions designed to guarantee the separation between secular and religious educational functions and to ensure that State financial aid supports only the former. All these provisions are precautions taken in candid recognition that these programs approached, even if they did not intrude upon, the forbidden areas under the Religion Clauses. We need not decide whether these legislative precautions restrict the principal or primary effect of the programs to the point where they do not offend the Religion Clauses, for we conclude that the cumulative impact of the entire relationship arising under the statutes in each State involves excessive entanglement between government and religion.

Excessive Entanglement

In *Walz v. Tax Commission*, the Court upheld state tax exemptions for real property owned by religious organizations and used for religious worship. That holding, however, tended to confine rather than enlarge the area of permissible state involvement with religious institutions by calling for close scrutiny of the degree of entanglement involved in the relationship. The objective is to prevent, as far as possible, the intrusion of either into the precincts of the other.

Our prior holdings do not call for total separation between church and state; total separation is not possible in an absolute sense. Some relationship between government and religious organizations is inevitable. *Zorach v. Clauson*, (1952); *Sherbert v. Verner*, (1963). Fire inspections, building and zoning regulations, and state requirements under compulsory school-attendance laws are examples of necessary and permissible contacts. Indeed, under the statutory exemption before us in *Walz*, the State had a continuing burden to ascertain that the exempt property was in fact being used for religious worship. Judicial caveats against entanglement must recognize that the line of separation, far from being a "wall," is a blurred, indistinct, and variable barrier depending on all the circumstances of a particular relationship.

This is not to suggest, however, that we are to engage in a legalistic minuet [a complex dance] in which precise rules and forms must govern. A true minuet is a matter of pure form and style, the observance of which is itself the substantive end. Here we examine the form of the relationship for the light that it casts on the substance.

In order to determine whether the government entanglement with religion is excessive, we must examine the character and purposes of the institutions that are benefited, the nature of the aid that the State provides, and the resulting relationship between the government and the religious authority. MR. JUSTICE [JOHN] HARLAN, in a separate opinion in *Walz*, supra [see above mention], echoed the classic warning as to "programs, whose very nature is apt to entangle the state in details of administration. . . ." Here we find that both statutes foster an impermissible degree of entanglement.

Rhode Island Program

The District Court made extensive findings on the grave potential for excessive entanglement that inheres in the religious character and purpose of the Roman Catholic elementary schools of Rhode Island, to date the sole beneficiaries of the Rhode Island Salary Supplement Act.

The church schools involved in the program are located close to parish churches. This understandably permits convenient access for religious exercises since instruction in faith and morals is part of the total educational process. The school buildings contain identifying religious symbols such as crosses on the exterior and crucifixes, and religious paintings and statues either in the classrooms or hallways. Although only approximately 30 minutes a day are devoted to direct religious instruction, there are religiously oriented extracurricular activities. Approximately two-thirds of the teachers in these schools are nuns of various religious orders. Their dedicated efforts provide an atmosphere in which religious instruction and religious vocations are natural and proper parts of life in such schools. Indeed, as the District Court found, the role of teaching nuns in enhancing the religious atmosphere has led the parochial school authorities to attempt to maintain a one-to-one ratio between nuns and lay teachers in all schools, rather than to permit some to be staffed almost entirely by lay teachers.

On the basis of these findings the District Court concluded that the parochial schools constituted "an integral part of the religious mission of the Catholic Church." The various characteristics of the schools make them "a powerful vehicle for transmitting the Catholic faith to the next generation." This process of inculcating religious doctrine is, of course, enhanced by the impressionable age of the pupils, in primary schools particularly. In short, parochial schools involve substantial religious activity and purpose. . . .

Pennsylvania Program

The Pennsylvania statute also provides state aid to church-related schools for teachers' salaries. The complaint describes an educational system that is very similar to the one existing in Rhode Island. According to the allegations, the church-related elementary and secondary schools are controlled by religious organizations, have the purpose of propagating and promoting a particular religious faith, and conduct their operations to fulfill that purpose. Since this complaint was dismissed for failure to state a claim for relief, we must accept these allegations as true for purposes of our review.

As we noted earlier, the very restrictions and surveillance necessary to ensure that teachers play a strictly nonideological role give rise to entanglements between church and state. The Pennsylvania statute, like that of Rhode Island, fosters this kind of relationship. Reimbursement is not only limited to courses offered in the public schools and materials approved by state officials, but the statute excludes "any subject matter expressing religious teaching, or the morals or forms of worship of any sect." In addition, schools seeking reimbursement must maintain accounting procedures that require the State to establish the cost of the secular as distinguished from the religious instruction.

The Pennsylvania statute, moreover, has the further defect of providing state financial aid directly to the church-related school. This factor distinguishes both *Everson* and *Allen*, for in both those cases the Court was careful to point out that state aid was provided to the student and his parents—not to the church-related school.

Political Impact

A broader base of entanglement of yet a different character is presented by the divisive political potential of these state programs. In a community where such a large number of pupils are served by church-related schools, it can be assumed that state assistance will entail considerable political activity. Partisans of parochial schools, understandably concerned with rising costs and sincerely dedicated to both the religious and secular educational missions of their schools, will inevitably champion this cause and promote political action to achieve their goals. Those who oppose state aid, whether for constitu-

tional, religious, or fiscal reasons, will inevitably respond and
employ all of the usual political campaign techniques to prevail. Candidates will be forced to declare and voters to choose.
It would be unrealistic to ignore the fact that many people
confronted with issues of this kind will find their votes aligned
with their faith. . . .

The potential for political divisiveness related to religious
belief and practice is aggravated in these two statutory programs by the need for continuing annual appropriations and
the likelihood of larger and larger demands as costs and popu-
lations grow. The Rhode Island District Court found that the
parochial school system's "monumental and deepening financial crisis" would "inescapably" require larger annual appropriations subsidizing greater percentages of the salaries of lay
teachers. Although no facts have been developed in this respect in the Pennsylvania case, it appears that such pressures
for expanding aid have already required the state legislature to
include a portion of the state revenues from cigarette taxes in
the program.

Inevitable Progression Argument

In *Walz* it was argued that a tax exemption for places of religious worship would prove to be the first step in an inevitable
progression leading to the establishment of state churches and
state religion. That claim could not stand up against more
than 200 years of virtually universal practice imbedded in our
colonial experience and continuing into the present.

The progression argument, however, is more persuasive
here. We have no long history of state aid to church-related
educational institutions comparable to 200 years of tax exemption for churches. Indeed, the state programs before us
today represent something of an innovation. We have already
noted that modern governmental programs have self-
perpetuating and self-expanding propensities. These internal
pressures are only enhanced when the schemes involve institu-

tions whose legitimate needs are growing and whose interests have substantial political support. Nor can we fail to see that in constitutional adjudication some steps, which when taken were thought to approach "the verge," have become the platform for yet further steps. A certain momentum develops in constitutional theory and it can be a "downhill thrust" easily set in motion but difficult to retard or stop. Development by momentum is not invariably bad; indeed, it is the way the common law has grown, but it is a force to be recognized and reckoned with. The dangers are increased by the difficulty of perceiving in advance exactly where the "verge" of the precipice lies. As well as constituting an independent evil against which the Religion Clauses were intended to protect, involvement or entanglement between government and religion serves as a warning signal.

Finally, nothing we have said can be construed to disparage the role of church-related elementary and secondary schools in our national life. Their contribution has been and is enormous. Nor do we ignore their economic plight in a period of rising costs and expanding need. Taxpayers generally have been spared vast sums by the maintenance of these educational institutions by religious organizations, largely by the gifts of faithful adherents.

The merit and benefits of these schools, however, are not the issue before us in these cases. The sole question is whether state aid to these schools can be squared with the dictates of the Religion Clauses. Under our system the choice has been made that government is to be entirely excluded from the area of religious instruction and churches excluded from the affairs of government. The Constitution decrees that religion must be a private matter for the individual, the family, and the institutions of private choice, and that while some involvement and entanglement are inevitable, lines must be drawn.

Religious People Should Be Politically Active

Jerry Falwell

Urged on by prominent members of the Religious Right, Jerry Falwell founded the Moral Majority in 1979. The organization soon emerged as the leading voice for traditional values in American politics and is credited with delivering over two-thirds of evangelical votes to Ronald Reagan in the 1980 election. A long-time preacher at the Thomas Roads Baptist Church in Lynchburg, Virginia, Falwell had been apolitical for most of his career. In the following excerpt, he cites threats to the traditional American family, such as the acceptance of homosexuality and abortion, that convinced him to become more politically involved. He also sets forth a number of positions, on politics, government, and economics, which shaped his vision of the Moral Majority and his own role in public policy. The Moral Majority itself dissolved in 1989, giving way to the Christian Coalition, but Falwell remained a highly influential, and often controversial, figure in the Religious Right and Republican Party politics. He died in May 2007 in his office at Liberty University, which he had founded as Lynchburg Baptist College in 1971.

The traditional American family was being threatened by economic pressures, physical and emotional abuse, sexual immorality, and divorce. Illegal drugs and alcohol misuse were reaching epidemic proportions across the generations from elementary school through the adult years. Pornography had become a major American industry, and pornographic materials were flooding the mails and being sold to children in neighborhood grocery stores or shopping centers. And abortions in America would soon reach 1.5 million victims a year.

Jerry Falwell, from *Strength for the Journey: An Autobiography*, New York: Simon & Schuster, 1987, pp. 342–372. Copyright © 1987 by Reverend Jerry Falwell. All rights reserved. Reproduced by permission of Simon & Schuster Macmillan.

The general moral standards of an entire generation seemed to be lowering steadily, and the courts and the politicians seemed silent if not supportive of the dangerous and deadly trend.

I continued to preach and teach against abortion. As the Biblical truths and medical data became clearer in my mind, my sermons and lectures became more informed and more determined. As the horrifying information about the related crisis threatening the American family came pouring into my life, my focus widened and my commitment to Biblically based, thoroughly Christian social action deepened. I was calling my people at Thomas Road Baptist Church to action, and through our "Old Time Gospel Hour" national broadcast I was reaching out to other clergy and laity across the nation.

A Changed Emphasis

People were shocked and surprised by the changed emphasis they heard in my preaching. Until the 1970s I had been a typical Baptist pastor who was opposed to Christians, especially the clergy, getting involved in political action. Suddenly I was calling for all-out political involvement by the Christian community. I had read and reread the stories and the sermons of the Old Testament prophets and their call to justice. I had restudied the life and teachings of Jesus, with His love for the little children and His command to see that no harm should come to them. I read the letters of Paul, Peter, and John, the books of Acts and Revelation. I felt a growing commitment to take my stand prophetically against the influence of Satan in our nation and through our nation to the world.

In my book *If I Should Die Before I Wake* I retrace the history of God's dealings with me about the abortion issue. I don't want to repeat that whole story here. I will only share one brief Biblical account that God used to help set me in my new direction. At the heart of my decision was a story repeated by Matthew, Mark, and Luke in their New Testament accounts of the life and teachings of Jesus. In Matthew 22, Mark 12, and Luke 20, the eyewitnesses document what happened that day when Jesus's enemies, the Pharisees, gathered to trick and trap Him in a public debate.

Is it lawful to pay taxes to Caesar, or not? the Pharisees asked, looking around at the crowd, knowing that either way Jesus answered He would be in trouble. If He answered, No, don't pay taxes to the government, the soldiers would arrest Him and throw Him in jail. If He answered, Yes, pay your taxes, He would offend the people who hated the government and wanted to see it overthrown. Jesus didn't answer immediately. Instead, He called for a Pharisee to hold up a coin used in paying the tax.

Whose image and inscription is this? Jesus asked.

Caesar's, answered the Pharisees.

"Render to Caesar the things that are Caesar's," Jesus replied, "and to God the things that are God's."

Two Different Worlds

On the surface, it was a clever answer. Both sides were satisfied. But it wasn't only clever. It was wise and true and filled with meaning. Jesus's answer cut to the heart of our human predicament. We live in two different worlds simultaneously. The world that God is building in the heart of men and women is an invisible world based on eternal values. The world that man is building is a world of cement, steel, and glass based on human values that rust, corrupt, and die.

The trouble is that we live in both worlds at the same time. We who are committed to the invisible world of God and to His values cannot simply stand aside while the other world destroys itself and the world we share. In that confrontation with the Pharisees, Jesus also reminded us subtly that though our first allegiance is to God and to His goals for this planet, we must still be responsible citizens, willing to play our part in maintaining the world of humankind.

There was a second important reminder for me in that story. When Jesus said, "Render to Caesar the things that are Caesar's, and to God the things that are God's," He was not just telling us to be responsible in both worlds. He was also reminding us that we live in two worlds simultaneously and that we need to keep the worlds apart. Each world works differently. What we do in God's world and with His people has different rules from what we do in the world of government, with elected officials and volunteers. America is not a theocracy, a government with God as its Commander-in-Chief. America is a democratic republic with a man (perhaps one day a woman) as its chief executive officer. In God's world, we decide by God's rules. In a democratic republic, we work together, governed by the will of the majority. In God's world, we submit to Him. In man's world we submit to God and to the law of man.

Precedence of God's Law

But there is a third important truth implied in Jesus's simple story. Jesus made this third truth clear by the example He set in His life and by His death. God used this third truth to challenge me to political action. Although we live in two worlds simultaneously and although both worlds are to be kept separate, when there is a conflict between the worlds, the world of God takes precedence over the world of man. When we feel the law of man is unjust or contrary to the law of God, we work to change man's law. And if the law of man actually comes into conflict with the law of God, we disobey man's law and pay the penalty.

We cannot forget God's law as we live in man's world. We must try to live by God's law in both worlds, whatever it may cost us. We must work to convince others that God's law is right and will bring health and long life to the nation. We do not insist on others believing as we believe or worshipping as we worship. We protect the freedom of every person in the land. But if we feel a law is wrong or harmful for the nation, we must work tirelessly to change it. And we must use every legal tool available to us to accomplish that end.

Duty to Political World

During my first years of ministry, I had given to God what was God's and had almost eliminated my responsibility to Caesar (government) altogether. I had paid my taxes, of course. I had voted. I had occasionally made a call or written a letter or carried on a conversation to influence public policy. From time to time my sermons commented on issues of significance to the nation. But to work hard to change public policy or to dedicate time and energy to influence government regarding abortion, the destruction of the family, alcohol and drug abuse, national defense, pornography, and general moral decay would be a new and mind-boggling experience for me.

I was already preaching national repentance and individual spiritual revival and renewal from my pulpit at Thomas Road Baptist Church. And I was speaking against abortion through our radio and television programs to homes across the nation. It wasn't enough.

I began to urge my fellow Christians to get involved in the political process. I encouraged them to study the issues, to support qualified candidates who stood for the renewal of morality and good sense in the land, or to run for office themselves. I pushed for Christians to use their churches to register voters. I dared Christians to go door-to-door getting out the vote, making the issues known, campaigning precinct-by-precinct for the candidates of their choice and using their cars and buses to get voters to the polls. . . .

Primary Concerns

The university students consistently ask the same questions and invariably they are surprised to hear my answers:

1. I did not found the Moral Majority to enshrine into law any set of fundamentalist Christian doctrines. Roman Catho-

lics make up at least 30 percent of our membership. Other members come from almost every Protestant denomination, and there are Mormons, Jews, agnostics, and atheists as well.

2. I oppose abortion but I would accept legislation that would permit abortion for women who are victims of incest or rape or in pregnancies where the life of the mother is at stake.

3. Although I believe that sexual intercourse belongs in a loving, caring monogamous family relationship, I do not oppose birth control in this free, pluralistic society. And though many of my Catholic brothers and sisters in the Moral Majority disagree with me here, I personally favor the use of appropriate birth control methods in the prevention of unwanted pregnancies.

4. Although I see homosexual practice as a moral wrong and do not favor their being singled out as a specially protected minority, I do not want to deny homosexual men or lesbian women their civil rights or take away their right to accommodations or employment or even their right to teach in public schools as long as they don't use the classroom to promote homosexuality as an alternative lifestyle.

5. I support absolute equal rights for women. But I opposed the Equal Rights Amendment as flawed and not the appropriate or necessary tool to achieve that full equality.

6. I oppose the world's growing stockpile of nuclear arms and I fear its eventual use in the destruction of much of God's creation, but I believe in the development and maintenance of the strongest possible national defense as a deterrent to war. I am also opposed to any steps we might take toward unilateral disarmament or non-verifiable bilateral disarmament.

7. I want our children to be able to pray in their schools but I believe that the prayers should be voluntary, nonsectarian, and that no public official should write or mandate a prayer. Further, no child should be intimidated or embarrassed for not participating.

8. I believe in a pluralistic, democratic society where all the people are free to speak, where the majority rules but where no minority is exploited or discriminated against, where every race, color, or creed has equal access to justice and opportunity, where no one needs to be poor or hungry or afraid.

9. I do not believe in book burning or censorship of any kind. The press has often accused me of book burning. It isn't true. It has never been true. Our library at Liberty University has or will have every book by every author that any great university might have to support its academic offerings. We have a matchbook we distribute to make our point. "Moral Majority Book Burning Matches," the cover reads, with our logo emblazoned in red, white, and blue. "See official book list inside." When you open the matchbook to see the books we recommend burning, you will find a blank list and the words "That's right, there aren't any!"

10. I believe in America's unswerving support of the state of Israel and of the support of Jewish people everywhere. But I believe equally in working for peace in the Middle East, in respecting and supporting our Arab friends and allies, and in assisting the poor, the hungry, the dispossessed, and the homeless of that troubled region in every way we can.

11. I believe that we should go all out to control the illegal flood of harmful drugs into this country and to do everything possible to stop their use among our people. Drug dealers should face stiff sentences and heavy fines for their crime. Drug addicts should be given every possible assistance in overcoming their addiction.

12. I believe in the free enterprise system. I have seen the options and found them wanting. I look on socialism as mutually shared poverty. But I also believe that we must continue to struggle to bring justice, equality and a fuller measure of mercy and generosity through our free enterprise system. The exploitation of workers, the misuse and abuse of power and

wealth, the unequal and discriminatory distribution of profits should have no place in America's practice of capitalism.

Chronology

1620

Religious radicals, known as Puritans, settle in what is now Massachusetts. They draft the Mayflower Compact, which proclaims their journey had been "undertaken for the glory of God, and advancement of the Christian faith," with the purpose of forming a "civil body politic."

1636

Roger Williams, a clergyman who supported religious freedom and the separation of church and state, is banished from the Massachusetts Bay Colony. He establishes Providence, Rhode Island, which becomes known as a haven of religious liberty.

1681

William Penn, a Quaker convert, founds Pennsylvania. The colony becomes home not only to Quaker minorities, but also to a wide range of other religious groups unwelcome in other colonies. Penn drafts a colonial constitution, the Frame of Government, which codifies principles of religious liberty and the balancing of power across different branches of government.

1779

Thomas Jefferson writes the Virginia Statute for Religious Freedom, which forbids the government from dictating religious beliefs, stating that "Almighty God hath created the mind free" and "civil rights have no dependence on our religious opinions, any more than our opinions in physics or geometry."

1787

The U.S. Constitution is completed and Article Six states that "no religious test shall ever be required as a qualification to any office or public trust under the United States."

1791

Congress ratifies the Bill of Rights, whose First Amendment declares that "Congress shall make no law respecting an establishment of religion, or prohibiting the free exercise thereof." This becomes the foundation of constitutional law concerning the separation of church and state and the freedom of worship.

1802

In a letter to the Danbury Baptist Association, Thomas Jefferson first uses the phrase "building a wall of separation between church and state" to describe the First Amendment.

1827

Presbyterian minister Ezra Stiles Ely preaches "The Duty of Christian Freemen to Elect Christian Rulers," a sermon calling for the election of candidates who "know and believe the doctrines of our holy religion."

1833

The Commonwealth of Massachusetts officially withdraws support of an established church. It is the last state to do so.

1835

The Michigan legislature adopts an amendment to their constitution declaring the separation of church and state, the first to do so upon becoming a state.

1838

The Roman Catholic bishop of New York City lobbies for government funding of the city's Catholic schools. In 1894 New York adopts constitutional language prohibiting the state from funding sectarian schools.

1876

Congress requires that every state admitted to the Union after 1876 put a provision in its constitution stating that it would maintain a public school system "free from sectarian control."

1928

Al Smith, the Democratic governor of New York, becomes the first Roman Catholic to become a major party's nominee for president.

1947

In *Everson v. Board of Education*, the Supreme Court rules 5-4 that government funding to transport students to and from parochial schools does not violate the First Amendment. But this decision also said the Founders intended a "wall of separation" between church and state. "Neither a state nor the Federal Government can set up a church. Neither can pass laws which aid one religion, aid all religions or prefer one religion to another."

1954

Congress adds the words "under God" to the Pledge of Allegiance.

1956

A federal law establishes "In God We Trust" as the official motto of the United States.

1960

John F. Kennedy, a Catholic, states in a speech: "I believe in an America where the separation of church and state is absolute, where no Catholic prelate would tell the president (should he be Catholic) how to act, and no Protestant minister would tell his parishioners for whom to vote." Kennedy wins the presidential election.

1962

In *Eagle v. Vitale*, the U.S. Supreme Court prohibited prayer in the public schools as a way to prevent "the indirect coercive pressure" that occurs "when the power, prestige and financial support of government is placed behind a particular religious belief."

1976

Jimmy Carter, a born-again Christian, is elected president of the United States, bringing evangelical faith into the political spotlight.

1979

Televangelist Jerry Falwell founds the Moral Majority, a conservative Christian political organization that opposes abortion, gay rights, the Equal Rights Amendment, and arms talks with the Soviet Union.

1987

The Supreme Court throws out a ban by the Los Angeles airport on leafleting by members of Jews for Jesus, allowing religious expression in public or even government settings.

2000

Voters in California and Michigan rejected referenda that would have repealed church-state separation language in their constitutions and allowed the use of publicly funded vouchers for religious schools in their states.

2004

The U.S. Supreme Court, in *Locke v. Davey*, finds that Washington State may exclude theology students from receiving state-financed scholarships if they are pursuing a degree in devotional theology. Washington's Constitution prohibits financing of religious education, and a 1969 state code applies the prohibition to college financial aid.

Organizations to Contact

The editors have compiled the following list of organizations concerned with the issues debated in this book. The descriptions are derived from materials provided by the organizations. All have publications or information available for interested readers. The list was compiled on the date of publication of the present volume; the information provided here may change. Readers need to remember that many organizations take several weeks or longer to respond to inquiries.

American Atheists
PO Box 5733, Parsippany, NJ   07054-6733
(908) 276-7300
e-mail: info@atheists.org
Web site: www.atheists.org

American Atheists is dedicated to working for the civil rights of Atheists, promoting separation of state and church, and providing information about Atheism. It publishes the magazine *American Atheist: A Journal of Atheist News and Thought*, and has published over 120 books including Madalyn Murray O'Hair's *Why I Am an Atheist*.

American Center for Law and Justice (ACLJ)
Web site: www.aclj.org

The American Center for Law and Justice (ACLJ) focuses on constitutional law and is based in Washington, D.C. The ACLJ is specifically dedicated to the ideal that religious freedom and freedom of speech are inalienable, God-given rights. The Center's purpose is to educate, promulgate, conciliate, and where necessary, litigate, to ensure that those rights are protected under the law. The ACLJ web site offers various multimedia including news releases, commentaries, and podcasts.

American Civil Liberties Union (ACLU)

125 Broad St., 18th Fl., New York, NY   10004-2400

(212) 549-2500

e-mail: aclu@aclu.org

Web site: www.aclu.org

The ACLU is a national organization that works to defend civil rights as guaranteed in the Constitution. Accordingly, it supports a strict separation of government and religion. It publishes various materials on civil liberties and a set of handbooks on individual rights.

Americans for Religious Liberty (ARL)

PO Box 6656, Silver Spring, MD   20916

(301) 598-2447

Web site: www.arlinc.org

Americans for Religious Liberty (ARL) is an educational organization that works to preserve religious, intellectual, and personal freedom in a secular democracy. It advocates the strict separation of church and state. ARL publishes numerous pamphlets on church/state issues and the quarterly newsletter *Voice of Reason*.

Americans United for Separation of Church and State

518 C Street NE, Washington, DC   20002

(202) 466-3234

e-mail: americansunited@au.org

Web site: www.au.org

Americans United for Separation of Church and State is non-sectarian and nonpartisan group whose purpose is to protect separation of church and state by working on a wide range of pressing political and social issues. It publishes the magazine *Church & State*, and also produces issue-papers and reference materials.

American Vision
3150A Florence Rd. SW, Ste. 2, Powder Springs, GA   30127
(770) 222-7266
e-mail: avpress@mindspring.com
Web site: www.americanvision.org

American Vision is a Christian educational organization working to build a Christian civilization. It believes the Bible ought
to be applied to every area of life, including government.
American Vision publishes the monthly newsletter *Biblical
Worldview*.

Christian Coalition of America
PO Box 37030, Washington, D.C.   20013-7030
(202) 479-6900
e-mail: Coalition@cc.org
Web site: www.cc.org

The organization is one of the largest and most active conservative grassroots political organizations in America. The site
has news, articles, and information about issues of interest to
conservative Christians. It also provides information on how
Christians can become involved in the political process, join
local Christian Coalition chapters, and contact legislators regarding legislation of interest to conservative Christians. The
Christian Coalition of America also publishes the weekly newsletter *Washington Weekly Review*, which can be viewed on the
web site.

Ethics and Public Policy Center (EPPC)
1015 15th St. NW, Suite 900, Washington, DC   20005
(202) 682-1200
e-mail: Ethics@eppc.org
Web site: www.eppc.org

The Ethics and Public Policy Center (EPPC) is Washington,
D.C.'s premier institute dedicated to applying the Judeo-
Christian moral tradition to critical issues of public policy.
The EPPC deals openly and explicitly with religious and moral

issues in addressing contemporary issues, working to clarify the ways in which moral principles shape the choices that political leaders must make in our democracy. EPPC scholars write books, publish articles in the popular press and in scholarly journals, and appear frequently on television and radio. The EPPC web site offers an assortment of different publications, including the bi-weekly e-newsletter *EPPC Briefly*.

Freedom from Religion Foundation
PO Box 750, Madison, WI 53701
(608) 256-8900
e-mail: info@ffrf.org
Web site: www.ffrf.org

The Freedom from Religion Foundation is an educational group working for the separation of state and church. Its purposes are to promote the constitutional principle of separation of state and church, and to educate the public on matters relating to nontheism. It publishes the newspaper *Freethought Today*, as well as several books and brochures such as *The Case Against School Prayer*.

International Center for Law and Religious Studies
Brigham Young University, 452 JRCB, Provo, UT 84602
(801) 422-6842
e-mail: law_religion@byu.edu
Web site: www.iclrs.org

The International Center for Law and Religion Studies at Brigham Young University was founded in the late 1990s to promote freedom of religion and study the relations between governments and religious organizations. A main project of the Center is hosting an International Law and Religion Symposium. The annual symposium hosts over a hundred delegates from dozens of countries. The Center also runs *Religlaw*, an online document collection for laws respecting religion.

People for the American Way (PFAW)
2000 M St. NW, Ste. 400, Washington, DC   20036
(202) 467-4999
e-mail: pfaw@pfaw.org
Web site: www.pfaw.org

People for the American Way (PFAW) works to increase tolerance and respect for America's diverse cultures, religions, and values such as freedom of expression. It distributes educational materials, leaflets, and brochures. The PFAW web site also offers press releases, and an entire section dedicated to Freedom of Religion.

Unitarian Universalist Association of Congregations: Washington Office for Advocacy (UUA)
1320 18th Street NW, Suite 300B, Washington, DC   20036
(202) 296.4672
Web site: www.uua.org

The Unitarian Universalist Association supports of the separation of church and state in relation to public education, partisan politics, free exercise and religious pluralism, and encourages the maintenance of a public education system free of religious influences including prayer in schools and the inclusion of creationism in scientific textbooks. The web site has an online bookstore which offers a wide variety of publications.

For Further Research

Books

Robert S. Alley, ed., *The Supreme Court on Church and State*. New York: Oxford University Press, 1990.

Stephen L. Carter, *The Culture of Disbelief*. New York: Basic Books, 1993.

Forrest Church, ed., *The Separation of Church and State: Writings on a Fundamental Freedom by America's Founders*. Boston: Beacon, 2004.

Charles W. Colson, *God and Government: An Insider's View on the Boundaries Between Faith and Politics*. Grand Rapids, MI: Zondervan, 2007.

Derek Davis and Barry Hankins, eds., *New Religious Movements and Religious Liberty in America*. 2nd ed. Waco, TX: Baylor University Press, 2003.

Joan DelFattore, *The Fourth R: Conflicts over Religion in America's Public Schools*. New Haven, CT: Yale University Press, 2004.

Daniel L. Dreisbach, *Thomas Jefferson and the Wall of Separation Between Church and State*. New York: New York University Press, 2002.

Peter Edge, *Religion and Law: An Introduction*. Burlington, VT: Ashgate, 2006.

William R. Estep, *Revolution Within the Revolution*. Grand Rapids, MI: Eerdmans, 1990.

Marvin Frankel, *Faith and Freedom: Religious Liberty in America*. New York: Hill and Wang, 1994.

Welton C. Gaddy, *Faith and Politics: What's a Christian to Do?* Macon, GA: Smyth and Helwys, 1996.

Edwin S. Gaustad *Roger Williams: Prophet of Liberty*. New York: Oxford University Press, 2001.

Philip Hamburger, *Separation of Church and State*. Cambridge, MA: Harvard University Press, 2002.

Charles C. Haynes, Sam Chaltain, and John E. Ferguson Jr., *The First Amendment in Schools: A Guide from the First Amendment Center*. Nashville, TN: First Amendment Center, 2003.

Hugh Heclo and Wilfred M. McClay, *Religion Returns to the Public Square: Faith and Policy in America*. Baltimore: Johns Hopkins University Press, 2003.

Frank Lambert, *The Founding Fathers and the Place of Religion in America*. Princeton, NJ: Princeton University Press, 2003.

Leonard W. Levy, *The Establishment Clause: Religion and the First Amendment*. New York: Macmillan, 1986.

Alf Mapp Jr., *The Faiths of Our Fathers: What America's Founders Really Believed*. Lanham, MD: Rowman & Littlefield, 2003.

Stephen V. Monsma and J. Christopher Soper, *Equal Treatment of Religion in a Pluralistic Society*. Grand Rapids, MI: Eerdmans, 1998.

Richard John Neuhaus, *The Naked Public Square: Religion and Democracy in America*. Grand Rapids, MI: Eeerdmans, 1986.

Mark A. Noll and Luke E. Harlow, *Religion and American Politics: From the Colonial Period to the Present*. New York: Oxford University Press, 2007.

Gregory Schaaf, *Franklin, Jefferson and Madison: On Religion and the State*. Santa Fe, NM: CIAC Press, 2004

Brendan Sweetman, *Why Politics Needs Religion: The Place of Religion in the Public Square*. Downers Grove, IL: InterVarsity, 2006.

Paul Weller, *Time for a Change: Reconfiguring Religion, State, and Society.* New York: T&T Clark, 2005.

Philip J. Wogaman, *Christian Perspectives on Politics.* Revised and Expanded ed. Louisville, KY: Westminster John Knox Press, 2000.

Periodicals

Barbara Amiel, "An Eternal Struggle Between Church and State," *Maclean's*, November 5, 2007.

Perry Bacon, "Rise of the Religious Left," *Time*, March 19, 2007.

Rob Carlson et al., "Discussion of a Mormon President?" *Christian Century*, November 13, 2007.

Ross Douthat, "The God Vote," *Atlantic Monthly*, September, 2004.

Daniel L. Dreisbach, "Wall of Separation: An Abused Metaphor," *Current*, December 2006.

M. Stanton Evans, "The True Wall of Separation," *American Spectator*, April 2007.

Ethan Fishman, "Unto Caesar," *American Scholar*, Autumn 2007.

Melinda Grube, "Belief and Unbelief Among Nineteenth-Century Feminists," *Free Inquiry*, Summer 2003.

Stan Guthrie, "The Faith of Our Founders," *Christianity Today*, July 2006.

Kevin J. Hasson, "The Myth," *American Spectator*, February 2008.

Chris Hedges, "Christianizing U.S. History," *Nation*, January 28, 2008.

Donald Kennedy, "Science and God in the Election," *Science*, January 4, 2008.

James Kurth, "Religion and National Identity in Europe and America," *Society*, September 2007.

Edward J. Larson, "Declarations of Faith," *Time*, November 12, 2007.

Wilfred M. McClay, "Secularism, American Style," *Society*, September/October 2007.

Jon Meacham, "Golly, Madison," *Newsweek*, March 17, 2008.

Jon Meacham and Sarah Kliff, "A New American Holy War," *Newsweek*, February 17, 2007.

Lisa Miller, "In Defense of Secularism," *Newsweek*, February 25, 2008.

National Review, "Secularism and Its Discontents," December 27, 2004.

Mark Noll, "America's Two Foundings," *First Things*, December 2007.

James E. Parco and Barry S. Fagin, "The One True Religion in the Military," *Humanist*, September/October 2007.

Hanna Rosin, "Closing the God Gap," *Atlantic Monthly*, January/February 2007.

Andrew Stephen, "How Would Jesus Vote?" *New Statesman*, February 4, 2008.

John Tomasin, "Clear Proof America Is Not a 'Christian Nation,'" *Free Inquiry*, February/March 2008.

Garry Wills, "Romney and JFK: The Difference," *New York Review of Books*, January 17, 2008.

Robert Wuthnow, "Divided We Fall: America's Two Civil Religions," *Christian Century*, April 20, 1988.

Philip Yancey, "Church in State," *Christianity Today*, March 2008.

Index